Fuzzy Logic

*The Human Condition
as Viewed by Fuzzy the Cat* ™

Front and back covers illustrated by
Abdón J. Romero

FUZZY LOGIC
The Human Condition as Viewed by Fuzzy the Cat ™
by M. D. Pueppke

ISBN: 0-9678352-1-6

For more information, please contact:
Health Trust International, Inc.
P.O. Box 2170
St. Augustine, Florida USA 32085

or visit us at: http://www.fuzzythecat.com

Fuzzy Logic

The Human Condition as Viewed by Fuzzy the Cat™

by M. D. Pueppke

Published by
Health Trust International, Inc.

Fuzzy Logic

Table of Contents

Dedicated to all the unloved and abused cats in the world...

"May you someday find a nice, safe
and warm home."

M. D. Pueppke

Silence is golden

You know what? I get the idea that humans spend too much time talking and analyzing and categorizing and postulating, and too little time just having a look around. Blah, blah, blah, blah.

Why so many words? We cats just hang out listening to all this supposed *intellectual interchange* sometimes, and well, I have to tell you, most of what we hear could be said with a minimum of half of the effort put forth—or even better yet, in a lot of cases, just best not said at all!

It's like the humans are afraid of "silence" or something. Why is that? Why is the *quiet human* attributed all sorts of crazy kinds of abnormalities?

"You're so quiet today...aren't you feeling well?" "Are you mad?" "Did you have a bad day?" "Don't you understand?" ("Are you stupid!") "Are you shy?"

And it's like you want to say, "Can't a person just have a moment or two for reflection once in a while?" Or maybe, "The truth of the matter is, what you're saying is so utterly ridiculous that it would be better to leave it unanswered in silence than to try to come up with any kind of semblance of a response that would possibly salvage your incoherence!"

You know what I mean. If there are no words emitted, it's automatically assumed that *something is wrong*. "Airhead" comes to mind. No *words* means all *air*! And in this case, air is *bad*, because it is that thing that we know is floating around everywhere, but we just can't seem to get a grip on it—and you know what they say about people who "don't have a grip on things"!

Air is *sneaky* too, as I found out that if you ignore it and cut it off, your eyes begin to bulge out like big glassy marbles! Like the time I saw this menacing plastic bag lurking about on the patio of my house. It was a tricky prey, suddenly rising up and moving to another part with no warning.

Well, hunched down low up front, I stalked it with all my concentration and in one fell swoop, grabbed that wispy demon and rammed my head inside, fangs a glaring, planning to put an end to its sorry existence with one quick lock of the jaws. Rather unexpectedly, I found that this plastic bag was actually some kind of more intelligent being with quite sophisticated defense mechanisms. To my surprise, I realized that its sinewy body had enveloped my mouth and cut off my contact with, yes, that invisible sneaky air we were talking about.

I hate to admit it, but I was at a loss for what to do because I was quickly getting the feeling that for all my super talents as supreme hunter, this wimpy-looking plastic thing seemed to be getting the best of me. And it had locked on to my head like a pliable vice and just wouldn't let go!

Fortunately, one of the "owners" had glanced out back and seen my predicament, and come running to poke a hole in the bag demon's body so I could gasp in that life-sustaining substance that I had been so cruelly deprived of.

The "owner," after freeing me completely from its deadly grip, was heard commenting something like, "Crazy cat, do you want to kill yourself playing with a plastic bag?" I wanted to explain that this had *nothing* to do with suicide and in fact had been part of a fierce battle with my trying to rid their patio of this floating, life-sucking beast! But, I felt so woozy from the struggle that I decided best to just chalk this up to experience with the conclusion that if a plastic bag invader should attempt to enter my space again sometime in the future, I should perhaps spend much more time planning a better offensive. This was not *at all* pleasing for a hunter-type who is accustomed to dominating his prey.

Anyway, we were talking about "silence" and "airheads" and all the crazy things that go along with that. Quite simply, humans need *noise*. Thank God I'm a cat and I don't have that kind of pressure put on me, even though the "owners" do get a little worried if I don't let out a few characteristic "meows" to show my verbal approval when the little round cans with fish in them are broken out at dinner time. I mean, if I just saunter into the kitchen and hang out for the food while making no sounds or circling movements, they begin to worry.

"What's wrong with Fuzzy?" "Isn't he feeling well?" "Is he mad?" "Did he have a bad day?" Amazing, isn't it!

I just wanna *eat*, that's all. Sometimes I feel like talking about it, and other times, I only want to get at those little cut-up fish and then go about my business. Do I *have* to give a full discourse before every meal even when we all know it's the same darn flavored fish in the same darn little round cans at the same darn time every night? I mean, what is there to say?

Once in a while, sure, I come in famished, and I'm meowing around saying, "Okay, hurry up, I'm really, really hungry and it smells great, and yeah, open it up faster and put it quickly in my dish, and no, you don't need to pet me, just put the dish on the floor, now, and let me get at it, and..."

But, other times, I just sort of eat more to please the "owners" than anything else. I used to not do that, but it resulted in all kinds of complications. This all relates to the misconceptions of that illusive "internal clock" many humans think they have figured out. You see, internal clocks are real, but they just don't work exactly the way one thinks.

To begin with, we cats are *extremely* well tuned in this sense. For example, we know when spring is coming before humans even have a clue about its arrival. I mean, humans sometimes try to evaluate weather patterns because certain temperatures and precipitation types supposedly indicate a change of seasons. Or, for the real erudites, they pull out their trusty calendars and declare that only on a certain day when the sun is doing who knows what over who knows where, then we can "officially" say that its "springtime."

There are even the more nostalgic and philosophical who suddenly get the "feeling" that "spring is around the corner," and this "feeling" is augmented by physical evidence of flowers blooming, birds singing, and something about this "air thing" again—coming in like a lion and going out like a lamb. I have no idea what they're talking about there. I do understand though that "lamb" comes in as a nice alternative to the little cut-up fish from time to time, but that's only hearsay in the neighborhood from some cat down the block who's got some ridiculously attentive "owners." As for "lions," I've been told they're just overgrown, lazy "Fuzzys" that don't even have their own houses or "owners" to watch over things for them. King of the *what*? You've gotta be kidding!

Let me put it to you in the easiest and most uncomplicated way I can—"spring is here," quite simply, when you get the insatiable and uncontrollable urge to go out howling at night in search of an exquisite feline of the female persuasion, and when the female feline, simultaneously tuning in, finds something extremely attractive and alluring in all this howling about in the wee hours of the morning!

Now is that so difficult to understand? We're not exactly talking "internal clock" here, but rather, full-scale whistles, drums, and alarm bells going off in an ear-piercing barrage! This is the sound of trumpets before marching into battle, the national anthem before the big game, the calm before the storm, the light at the end of the tunnel—this is, "Spring!"

Well, that's just one example of the famous "internal clock." At least after having read this far, you should now have some kind of confidence in cat climatology. Getting back to how I started this subject, this all has a lot to do with our eating habits too. In other words, we've all gotta eat to live—although in one of those "famished moods" like I mentioned earlier, it's more like "living to eat"—and the internal clock helps tell us when it's time to send down the little cut-up fish to that great stomach processing factory.

It's like a "fish alarm" that announces, "Get the little round can out of the cupboard *now* and don't keep Fuzzy waiting!" As each moment passes with inaction, the alarm becomes more penetrating and nerve-rattling, because hungry or not, it's *time*, and everybody knows it! This causes one to move about nervously in the house, hoping that someone is in the kitchen so the warning can be given in the appropriate location and action can be taken more quickly.

If the "owners" are found lazing about in the living room or another non-critical spot, the situation becomes much more dramatic because humans can—in their "untuned-in kind of way"—be completely oblivious to all this. Amazingly, the internal clock can be sounding off like the final round of fireworks on the Fourth of July and the "owners" might be discovered sitting about in casual conversation or watching some inane television program, as if we weren't about to reach the fail-safe point of no return!

My movements become more nervous with each passing moment, and I'm meowing to them, "Get up! Hurry! It's the fish alarm—come on! Look at my decaying physical condition! The fish, the little cut-up fish! Go to the kitchen! Can't you hear the alarm? It's time to eat! Follow me—I'll show you how to get to the kitchen. I know where you hid the little round cans—over this way, hurry! Oh, the alarm, we have to eat now...!"

Just my body language alone should be enough to tell them that this is a desperate situation and that time is of the essence. The "owners" typically linger about for a few minutes and then suddenly, as if this were a first time occurrence and didn't happen every night of the week and every day of the year (!), will say something like, "Oh, do you want to eat, Fuzzy?" And I meow back, "Let's get serious here—what do you think I've been telling you for the last half hour!"

I could of course be a lot more sarcastic and derogatory at this point, but logic tells me there is some connection between my eating cut-up fish and the humans' willingness to free it from its round-canned prison, so best to stay cool and do a couple of rubs up against their legs in appreciation for their kind participation in this stressful moment.

Now if I don't happen to be in one of those "famished" moods, this is when the problems can crop up. You see, this is the misunderstanding of the internal clock—it tells you that it's *time to eat* and that this critical moment must be adhered to with a religious punctuality, but it does not make any mention of *how hungry* you might be or not. And therein, lies the catch.

Sometimes, after all my advanced antics to get them into the kitchen—in respect for the sacred hour of dinner—to be quite honest, I'm just not very hungry at all. The point is—and this is the crux of the matter—it's not *how much* you eat, but rather the fulfilling of the serving of the cut-up fish at the *scheduled time* that is important. The problem is, the "owners" just don't see it that way.

For example, some evenings, after much struggle and acrobatics, I will have finally gotten them into the kitchen to serve my dinner. At that point, the piercing alarm of the internal clock shuts off, my stress level goes way down, and I might just simply sniff the food a little, take a bite or two, and then walk off feeling completely satisfied. Mission accomplished, right? Believe it or not, for some strange reason, this sends them into hysterics!

"You mean you caused all that commotion and aggravation just to sniff your food and then you're not even going to eat!" And they huff and puff about the kitchen as if something were seriously wrong.

I try to explain that everything is just great. That *we*, as a *team*, conquered the internal clock and once again freed the fish from its shiny cage. That *we* had fulfilled our daily calling of the kitchen ritual and that *we* should feel honored and pleased to have partaken in such a noble cause.

"Baloney," they say, "if that's the way you're going to behave, then we'll just see how you like going back to *dry* food!"

Ouch—that was a blow below the belt! *Dry* food! I heard they serve that stuff to *dogs* or other *inferior* species, but we're talking about *felines* here! This is *Fuzzy's* palate we're concerned about!

Well, at that point, I usually have to make my way, half-heartedly, back into the kitchen and try to eat enough to make it look like I had an appetite, and then plod out a few minutes later with everyone in a rather foul mood—the "owners" for my "bad behavior" and me, with an indigestion that maybe even the best clump of sweet bluegrass may not take away. You see what us cats have to put with!

What can I say—it's a strange world. Like when the human "lady owner" comes back to my house and I'm dozing off and she is the only one home at the moment. She'll typically greet me (better said—wake me!) with something mundane like, "Oh, Fuzzy, *sleeping* again, you lazy cat!"

Like, what does she expect me to be doing all day—composing a new piano concerto or studying advanced electronics? Doesn't she know that we cats have pre-defined, duly ordained, inviolable daily missions that *require* us to cat nap a minimum of twelve to sixteen hours? Doesn't she know *who* made the expression "cat nap" famous? Isn't it obvious?

Anyway, she "booms in" and I usually get up, do one of those fantastically elegant hunch-back stretches we're so renowned for so as to get out the kinks, and then follow her around the house a little. It's sort of funny, but I heard her once tell a friend that, "My Fuzzy is so glad to see me come home that he gets right up to greet me and then follows me around like a lost soul!"

Can you believe that egotistical mush? The truth of the matter is that I just want to see if she's got any new cat toys or kitty snacks on her! But what the heck, I guess it's sort of good to have the "owner" back in my domain too.

What she does next I just haven't really figured out yet. Normally, she'll mutter something like, "Oh Fuzzy, the house is so quiet!"—as if that weren't the perfect "napping" scenario—and then will proceed to turn on noise-making boxes. A typical day will have just the t.v. blasting its foul programming for all to hear, but sometimes she will even go to the bother of turning on the tube, with no volume, and then cranking up the stereo to ear-piercing levels at the same time!

What's going on here? I thought the best part of television was the visual images that get sucked into that lifeless window on the world, but then she'll be bopping from room to room without even looking at what's happening. And then, as if all sanity had been temporarily suspended, her putting on the stereo music *along with* the television programming leaves me completely speechless.

At first, I thought it was some kind of special joint media effort that she must have been informed about, so I sat down in front of the t.v. to watch what appeared to be a serious drama in a hospital room setting, while the stereo was blaring out something about "your Mama's gonna be hot tonight"! What does one thing have to do with the other? Is this some kind of top-secret, coded dialogue or am I just completely out of tune with the new media mergers?

No matter, because the "lady owner" is just as happy as can be, probably even humming something that goes neither with the t.v. nor stereo noise—or most likely, talking to me a mile a minute like I really cared about exactly how her day had gone.

She'll start out, "Fuzzy, you wouldn't believe what Janet told me today during the morning break!" I meow back, "It doesn't interest me in the slightest, but got any of those little bouncing balls on you that…?"

And she continues, "Well, it seems that Bill has been having an affair with Lucy. Can you believe that?" And I say, "That has *little* or probably *no* worldly importance, but I would like to know how the supply of little round cans of fish is holding up?"

And she insists, "And as if that weren't enough, it seems that Lucy might be pregnant!" I meow in return, "Now that is serious...another noise-making, gossiping, nap-disturbing human on the way into this world. I think that this Bill fellow has behaved very irresponsibly and should possibly be tortured until..."

The lady owner interrupts my thoughts and says, "But I have to admit, they do make a nice couple, even though Bill is still married to his third wife and Lucy already has four different children by four different men."

"My God!", I exclaim, getting caught up in the heat of the live office soap opera, "And you humans talk down the alley cats among us who just happen to be celebrating the arrival of 'spring' when this Bill and Lucy couple make the wildest cat's night out look like a boring walk in the park! We should have a *serious* talk with that floozy Lucy dame now, and let her know..."

"Oh, well," she sighs. "To each his own. Isn't that right, Fuzzy?"

"To each, his *what*? How can you get me all worked up over this story, when I was just innocently napping and minding my own business, and then just come out with, 'to each his own'? What does that mean? I say this Bill and Lucy need immediate therapy and that..."

"Do you know what else happened today, Fuzzy? You're not going to believe this!"

"Hey, wait a minute. Don't be changing subjects so fast here. I want to know what Bill's going to do if Lucy's really..."

It was a lost cause. She went on like that for the next fifteen or twenty minutes, starting out with these banal, oh-so-human topics and never letting me get the satisfaction of at least seeing one story line out to its logical conclusion. What can I say. It's all a part of the human "noise" that I've slowly—and with much difficulty—become accustomed to.

They say "silence is golden" you know. Maybe sometimes it's just better to know less than to know more, to see less than to see more, to hear less than to hear more. In other words, "less" is "more." Otherwise, it's just a lot of useless clutter that comes in the form of bits and pieces that never quite fit together anyway.

It's like you have two half-complete jigsaw puzzles with their stuff all scrambled into one. At first glance, you figure you still got a chance of completing the wonderful picture that comes on the box. But, after hours and hours of serious endeavor, you realize that the best you can do is create a sort of distorted countryside background with an incomplete high-speed racetrack, featuring a beautiful Ferrari car body with cow legs holding it up. Won't take you too far too fast, but at least it saves on tires and runs on grass.

You know what the *real* problem is? Under these circumstances, most humans will just arrive at the conclusion that they must have put the puzzle together wrong, and so will go at it again and again and again and again. There will be advanced-level consultations, high-level meetings, upper-level research—unfortunately, all to no avail because in this case, quite simply, the Ferrari body came with cow legs from the get-go.

It's like this—either live with it as it is, or start over at the factory. Sometimes there's no "in between." Sometimes there's no "if I just try a little harder, work a little longer—everything will be okay."

Some things are just plain screwed up and that's the way they're going to stay, like it or not.

Whatever you do, just don't talk to *me* about it, please! I really need to get more sleep. Yes, sleep more and talk less. Although I do sort of wonder what happened to Bill and Lucy...

How do I look?

Chapter Two

They wanted to give me a *bath*—can you believe that?!? "They"—the "owners"—in their infinite wisdom, had decided that "Fuzzy was looking a little scruffy," and besides, they were having some people over that night for a business dinner, so everything had to look just perfect! It's like, have you ever heard anyone say, "Well, George, the proposal looks great and the price is surely right, but that *scruffy-looking cat* of theirs has really made me have second thoughts about this whole deal!" Come on—give me a break!

First of all, anyone with brains, or without head-to-toe fully protective metal body armor, simply would not think of mixing a cat with water. It's just not done, okay!

We DON'T LIKE WATER—got it? Yeah, yeah, you can mention the few psychotic felines that actually swim a little and play with faucets and all that stuff, but those poor creatures are some kind of sick genetic mutations that unfortunately give the rest of us *normal* breeds a sort of wimpy reputation around the ole watering hole. We've got top-flight scientific committees formed at the international level that are specifically working on the reduction and/or elimination of this embarrassing and devious birth defect.

Anyway, what gives? Can't you see that we spend enormous

amounts of time *bathing ourselves*—even in those hard-to-reach places like the lower back and top of the head? You've gotta believe that we've got everything under control and are just as clean as we would *like* to be and *need* to be for any given moment!

You must be thinking of *dogs* when you're thinking of baths. You know—those gangly, odorous, woofing things that will run right through a muddy puddle as if it were nothing and then come rub up against you afterward, maybe even doing that full-body, head-to-tail, twist-and-spray shake that would make even the best lawn sprinklers proud.

Those are *dogs*, got it! They *always* smell bad and probably could use a bath every other hour of their sorry existence, but here we're talking about the slick, the clean, the well-groomed—the *cat!* "Bath" and "cat" make a very inharmonious combination—it just doesn't slide off the tongue like, "Let's give that *filthy mutt* a *bath* before he stinks up the whole neighborhood!"

With a cat, you should just naturally want to say something like, "Let's leave the lovely, elegant, and sweet-smelling *Fuzzy* to his own naturally refreshing grooming techniques while we keep all *dogs* out on the corner of the patio, far, far away from the more civilized and intelligent inhabitants within the dwelling."

Well, I'm sorry to tell you that the explanation didn't work. They were set on giving me a bath and there was just no logical argument in this world that was going to change their minds.

I knew it was coming when they both sort of inched their way up to me on the couch with this silly-looking half grin on their faces. "Okay, Fuzzy, we have a big surprise for you and you're really going to like this, especially when we're all done and you see how handsome you're going to be! And it's not going to hurt at all. It's just a little water and a little shampoo—oh yes, we got the *special* no-tears baby shampoo *just for you* on this very special occasion, and it has such a nice, pleasant odor that..."

And on and on they go, I believe really knowing all the while that whatever they say or however they approach this, World War III is about to commence. All this jibber-jabber probably has a calming effect on their nerves as they're trying to block out the possibly all-to-vivid images of the last time they got this wild hair about cat baths and the "man owner" claimed afterwards to have no feeling whatsoever in his left thumb for at least two weeks following. Yeah, the ravages of war.

"No tears shampoo"—like that was going to make everything just fine and dandy! Well, at exactly 4:26 p.m., the battle began. They grabbed me by the scruff of the neck—I hate when they know those good-grip kinds of places where we can't wriggle free very easily. I immediately went into my "sink the claws deep into the couch cushion" counter-technique and had the "lady owner" screaming for high heaven as they slowly pried me loose, paw by paw, along with a good part of the stuffing that had previously lain undisturbed therein.

That left them with that oh-so-dangerous flight to the bathroom as I was furiously waving all four paws madly about in all directions, claws fully extended, and at rather impressively random speeds. This was the "cat defense weapon" in all its terrifying glory!

They carried me off in a half-run with a look of panic on their faces—holding my body fully extended out from theirs like I was some kind of bomb that was about to explode. I went on flailing about, managing to catch and disintegrate a nice strip of their clothing from time to time.

As we got close to the bathroom door, I could see it was time for even stronger and more drastic measures. I let out the most ghastly howling sound—one of those that originates deep inside the stomach and bursts out in high-pitched shrieks of terror—hoping this last-minute diversionary tactic may unnerve them enough to loosen their grip for that critical second or two needed for escape.

Unfortunately for me *and* the "man owner," this sudden shrieking sound didn't loosen his grip, but did manage to scare the heebee jeebies out of him, causing him unconsciously to pull my body in close to his. To this day, I think he still has some faint markings of the five "stripes" I scrolled down his chest at that moment with my left, front paw. Don't get me wrong, I actually like my "owners" a lot, but as they say, "All is fair in love and war."

Well, we entered the dreaded bathroom, bathtub already deviously filled to cat-height with warm water, and "no tears" shampoo strategically located at the side. Yes, I could see clearly that this had all been pre-meditated. The owners now were looking extremely battle-worn with frayed nerves that made their eyes pop out big and round, sporting sweaty and torn clothing—a once-nice designer blouse for the "lady owner"—and well, I won't go into the "stripes" on the "man owner" that I alluded to before. I will tell you that he had tears in his eyes. It was a dramatic scene of great struggle and courage on all parts.

They rushed me inside in a last minute offensive toward the awaiting "tub of doom" and before I knew it, I was stiff as a board standing neck high in this disgusting wet, watery stuff. I couldn't even talk or struggle anymore. You see, water has this "freezing" effect on us cats where we become like motionless statues once the evil liquid has penetrated our fur and soaked down to the pores. And besides, we look so "uncool" when all wet like that, that we're just hoping to get out and groomed up again as fast as possible before any of the neighbor felines might happen to walk by. It's a terrible, and rather emotionally unnerving moment.

This could even be *totally* devastating under certain circumstances. Like what if another strange male cat entered my territory at that very moment and I had to go out and look tough and menacing to scare him off when I'm dripping from ear to paw? Yeah, right! I'd look like some wimpy, skinny rat that probably even the crickets would roll over and laugh at! Let's hope the neighborhood stays calm for at least the next half hour.

It all turned out okay I guess as I got myself groomed and back to my normal handsome—and fiercesome—self again and the "owners" said that I looked "just great." What does that mean anyway—"looking great"? Of course, as cats go, I know that I'm top-of-the-line in terms of muscular body features, sexy meows, and a super soft attractive coat, but that's just *natural* for me. I was born *perfect*—what can I say!

But, did you ever think about how much time and money and energy humans spend on this "how do I look" kind of thing? You see, I watch the "owners" in my spare time because quite frankly, they're the best entertainment around a good part of the day. This is especially true weekday mornings before going to work, which I've personally designated as the "human panic session."

It all begins when this nasty alarm thing goes off at some extremely unreasonable hour of the morning. At the critical moment, I'm usually comfortably sprawled out somewhere on the "owners" bed, ideally sharing a part of a pillow when I can silently and secretly negotiate the unattended free space at night. Suddenly, and always without warning, there's this frightful, ear-piercing, buzzing sound emanating from a normally harmless and rather innocent-looking box that sits on the night stand—all of which sends vibrations of panic from your nose right down to the tip of your tail.

What kind of evil box is that anyway? The rest of the day I see it shine some pretty blue numbers, and if the "owners" touch it in some special way, it even begins to sing or talk at times in quite a pleasant and soothing manner. But in the mornings, it's like the Jeckyll and Hyde phenomenon that's transformed into this screaming beast that scares the living daylights out of you.

I don't get it. They know the darn thing is awfully temperamental and that almost every morning without fail, it just goes crazy until you pound it back into submission again. Why don't they just get rid of it, like that living room lamp that I had to tangle with?

I guess I can tell you quickly about the lamp incident even though the "owners" still hold a grudge against my ridding the house of that infernal glowing object. You see, according to what I heard and understood in the yelling during the rather grand death blow that I laid upon it, it was one of those one-of-a-kind "designer" porcelain-type lighting devices. Who knows what all that means, but it appears they had somehow succumbed to its powers and didn't see it for what it really was—a beacon of invasion for crazy flying moths in the otherwise peaceful home environment.

I think we all know and accept that any flitting, direction-changing, visible flying object can simply not be tolerated when it enters one's territorial airspace. That has to be some kind of natural law, don't you think? And this lamp was like a super magnet for these irritating white-winged kami-kazis that invaded my living room each evening.

I often tried to warn them, "Don't turn it on! You know they're waiting for the signal for invasion! Don't do it!" But sure enough, it got a little dark—and like they couldn't move around without light or something (!)—they'd start the thing a glowing. A few minutes later, one of those wildly insane moths would come in at lightening speed and begin some demonic ritual of circling the "bulb master"—a sight that just activates every attack mechanism built into an expert hunter like me.

My usual response was to slink over towards the flying enemy, with sharp, short movements, eyes a bulging, with every muscle in my body tense and strained for the upcoming battle. I was in my best form as you can imagine—physically and mentally—to do away with the crazed beast, when normally one of the "owners" would see my approach and shout out, "No, Fuzzy!"

I figure the reaction either came from their being so overly impressed by my offensive that they just couldn't stand to see it through to the end, or that somehow the demon moth had silently communicated his wish to live to them in some mysterious way and they thus put an end to the surely fatal assault.

Well, one evening I was well into my approach when the usual "termination" command was given, but at that very moment the moth went into a special wide-flying loop and nearly crashed into my nose before heading back to the "bulb master."

That was too much—not only had it invaded my territorial airspace, but now it had made a very *personalized* bombardment on one of the most sensitive parts of my perfect feline physique!

Ignoring the looks of horror on the "owners'" faces, I lunged at the enemy with all my force, claws extended and fangs a gleaming, and in one fell swoop grabbed the invader with my famous left-hook and pounded it flat and flightless to the hard, wooden surface of the table below. Unfortunately, it seems my most noble and self-sacrificing attack brought down the lamp along with its crazed flitting worshiper, sending hundreds of little pieces of the formerly lit moth temple in all directions.

The "owners," after a few seconds of silence and profound shock, went into hysterics. I thought at first they were expressing emotions of joy and amazement that I could have both knocked out not only the invading enemy but the source of its intrusion at the same time. I must say, that's quite a feat, don't you think! A two-for-one, double-your-pleasure kind of deal from my point of view.

It turns out, they weren't in the least bit happy about my well executed, double-death blow. They actually *chased* me out of the living room and in the heat of the moment, threatened to kick me out of the house and give me away for adoption should I ever, ever do anything like that again!

That just goes to show what happens to rational thinking when the humans get upset. First of all, I hated to remind them that the house was *mine*, and furthermore, it's *I* who make the decision about who lives with whom! After all, I'm doing *them* the favor of letting *them* hang out with *me* in *my* abode and take pleasure in *my* company, but fortunately they came back to their senses the next day. I suppose I'll let them stay on and just chalk it up to experience on their part.

Getting back to the "human panic session" that the alarm box gets going every morning...you know, that's another little "household device" that I'm going to have to deal with on my own someday since they can't seem to get up the courage to stop its screaming once and for all.

Anyway, the box starts to bellow its hideous sounds and this forces the humans out of their peaceful slumber, bringing them to their feet in a rather uncoordinated and unsophisticated kind of way. (No super-impressive, elegant, full-body, hunched-back stretches from this species!)

The only good thing about this daily pandemonium is that it

always results in their eventually making their way to the kitchen to liberate some cut-up fish from one of those little round cans. I just wish we could do this without the unnerving shock treatment that comes from that Jeckyll and Hyde box.

Well, now I go into "observation mode" as the morning routine begins. There's really nothing else to do at that hour anyway with the exception, of course, of respecting the sacred kitchen ritual. And besides, they're quite a sight as the whole thing gets going in full motion.

I used to hang out more with the "man owner," but I've learned over time that his ceremonial "things to do" routine was really much less complicated and sophisticated than that of the "lady owner," so I've sort of redirected my attention to the one of more interest.

The "man owner" usually has arisen from the bed first as it is he who has had to bring his body into motion before the other in order once again to slay the screaming alarm box at his side. I give him a silent round of applause as he brings it back into submission each day.

He immediately stumbles off towards the kitchen in the worst kind of rambling, half-conscious walk, with the sole objective of bringing the coffee pot to life. I used to spring out of bed to follow him, thinking this was "little round can" time, but learned through experience that his mental operational level during those first few moments was well below anything that would possibly allow him to dominate one of those flip-top aluminum lids.

Also, in my excitement, I used to weave in and out of his legs as he made the approach to that great room of food activities, only learning that all that whirling around mixed rather badly with his fixed, glazed eyeballs. Unfortunately, this resulted in several incidents of his crashing into the walls or falling face down in the hallway trying to deal with my maneuvers. His loud, screaming reaction remained incoherent at that hour of the day, but I clearly got the idea that he preferred to make the first trip to the kitchen unaccompanied.

Well, that's okay. I'll just hang out with the lady owner then. Her first priority—the shower—because you gotta be *clean*, I mean, *really clean* all the time! I've never really heard humans say to each other, "Hey, how do I smell? Do I smell nice and fresh, or more like that raggedy mutt down the block?" But, I get the feeling that this question is always just hanging about on the tip of their tongues.

The shower itself is frightfully steaming, with water temperatures that would slide the fur right off us more delicate feline species. I overheard in a conversation once that this has something to do with regenerating the brain activity of the human in the early morning. It appears that if you scald the living daylights out of yourself, the shock vibrations transmitted back through the skin cells just pop on those electric circuits like wildfire and get the whole system fully operational in no time! Wow, then the cleaning routine also serves to "start your engines," as I heard once on some metal box with wheels racing program.

But, it's much more complicated than that. I snuck into the shower once during the day to see what this hot and wet little closet looked like when not triggered to attack. I have to tell you that it's fully and thoughtfully equipped with soap for the face, soap for the body, soap for the (itching) feet, liquid soap for the hair, another liquid creamy soap for the hair—it was a soap emporium! A soap-lover's dream come true! A soap temple! A specially designed soap-filled chamber where not even the nastiest and most villainous dirt could possibly think of surviving. Where "clean" would reign and dominate for all those who dared to enter this watery retreat. It was a five-minute, steaming, bubbling, lathering sanctuary of odorous delight!

We still have a long way to go in the morning preparation process, as I learned, because "clean" doesn't necessarily mean that you "smell good," and "smelling good" doesn't always result in "looking good." You see, there are more steps to follow here before the human is really ready to come face-to-face with the oh-so-observant outside world. Pay attention now.

The "lady owner" gets out of the shower, brain waves humming more or less in unison and her entire body fully scrubbed and sparkling. After drying off, she immediately goes to the control-and-command center that is fully stocked with all the latest weaponry in deodorants, cosmetics, creams, and other advanced chemicals and solutions. I have to tell you, it's an impressive sight!

She begins her task with an efficiency and speed that could only come from years of training and practice. Key body parts are effectively masked with the most pleasant-smelling liquids. The eyes are accentuated so that they almost communicate with you without words. The cheeks are softened and smoothed as would be fit for a Greek Goddess. The lips are brilliantly colored in such a fashion that seems to make them offer themselves as a luscious garden of tropical fruit. A variety of special volcanic, herbal, and other creams are generously applied to various parts of the arms, hands, thighs, and stomach so as to smooth any devious wrinkles and reduce any attempt of fatty-cell invasion.

And then there's the hair! This may be the culmination and glory of the human body preparation as it is at the same time both the most psychologically sensitive part of the physical adornment and perhaps the most unruly and disconcerting aspect.

I've heard her grumble that, "Some days, I just can't do anything with it!" This makes me think that it somehow takes on a life of its own and when in that obstinate mode, will refuse to be combed, brushed, or blown into any satisfactory shape—at least through the eyes of the beholder. Hair must be extremely moody, and subject to the whims of some external or internal force that humans have yet to master. The biggest challenges of life can sometimes be the most innocent things, don't you think?

Okay, the body of the "lady owner" has been sufficiently cleaned, groomed, and covered so as to give her some degree of self-satisfaction. Now comes the second most difficult task of the morning after the skirmish with the hair—selecting the clothing!

Knowing the anxiety involved, I used to try to lend her a paw in this area by strolling into her closet and grabbing on to a blouse or skirt that I thought looked comfortable with one of my claws. If I tugged real hard, I could even manage to yank it off the hanger at times.

It appears my efforts weren't appreciated and she really wanted to make the decision alone because any selection on my part always resulted in, "Oh, Fuzzy, *no*! You're going to *ruin* my clothing!"

What's the deal? I *washed* my paws recently, and no one ever said that I didn't have a lot of *class* in my own daily appearance!

Anyway, she might go through two or three outfit changes before actually being able to make way for the kitchen, and even at that point, I always get the feeling that she never ever walked away from that closet completely satisfied with the combination of things she had put on!

Thank God I was born a *cat* and don't have to change *furs* every morning! "Now will that be calico or striped today? White 'booty' paws, or feet matching the leg fur? White 'tuxedo chest' or mixed colors?" Ridiculous, isn't it! Did you see my picture? Now who would want to change *perfection* like that! You just gotta leave a good thing alone!

The "man owner," well, he's sort of a boring "watch" after seeing what the "lady owner" puts herself through each morning. I mean, in terms of sophistication, advanced body preparation elements, efficiency, effectiveness, patience, style—you name it—she's got him hands down, cold in the water, down-and-out, no chance, no-way-José at the control-and-command center.

The shower thing might not be so different—especially in relation to the steam-charged brain activation—but what happens after is all speed and no style. He quickly throws on a little odor-masking stuff, tries to get his hair in order with some brute comb that has half its teeth missing, plops on the first thing that he sees in the closet, takes a quick look in the mirror where he clearly and consciously recognizes himself as the spitting image of Mr. Universe, and then heads on out of the bathroom ready to take on the world.

The lady will invariably ask the man, "How do I look?" The man, amazingly and without even having turned around, will often say something like, "You look just great, dear!" I've heard the expression about *having eyes in the back of one's head*, but I never really believed it until I got involved in the morning routine at my house. Pretty impressive, huh! I think that sort of gets the man some "points" back from what he lost in his lousy bathroom performance.

And you know, the man, for some reason, never asks the lady, "How do I look?" It's like the lady goes out half-assured that she put herself together right when in reality she could conquer the Roman Empire with just a fleeting glance or scent, and the man goes out convinced of victory before the battle has even begun, not realizing that he's missing a good part of his armor! It's a strange kind of mixed-up thing that quite frankly I may never figure out.

Well, after all that commotion, both finally make their way to the kitchen to chug down a couple of liquids and cram down a little sustenance before each goes out running to their respective metal boxes with wheels on them and heads off to something called "work." (I'll see if I can explain this strange concept a little later on.) By the time of their leaving, I've been properly supplied with a little round can of cut-up fish inside and am feeling quite satisfied for having successfully completed another morning routine with my frantic, but extremely well organized human "owners."

It's now time for me to clean myself up with a full head-to-tail licking, although not getting involved in the steamy shower, cosmetics, and other stuff that the "owners" feel obliged to partake in. Us cats just keep it simple and down to basics, but after all, it is sort of hard to improve on perfection. We just maintain the status-quo of appearance, knowing that, with the exception of that image-wrecking watery liquid, we'd look great with almost no effort at all!

Nap time. No doubt about it. I'd been up a little more than an hour, had eaten, and well, that was about enough strenuous activity for any feline without thinking about getting a little shuteye. I don't want to overdo it now, do I? I'll need my strength later on in the day for cricket hunting, territorial patrol, furniture scratching, and other important activities.

Oh yeah, there's a favorite spot on the corner of the couch where all the nice, soft cushions clump up together. Let me just curl up for a little while here and have a good, long rest. Hmmm, it's great to lie down, and yes, this is really soft and comfortable. That feels nice, I think I'll...

It was a dark, cold, blustery winter day in the Feline Kingdom. All the cat inhabitants had lived well and in peace since the dramatic defeat of the horrific "Doberman" almost two years ago. Fuzzy the Great, the most renowned and respected warrior ever to set paws on earth, had spent the many months since his triumphant battle with the "Doberman" in a comfortable retirement in his luxurious castle surrounded by a very well-stocked fish mote.

Yes, life was good. This was a cat's world, where cats assumed their natural role of terrestrial domination and control, where mice were abundant and didn't run too fast, where fish were plentiful and didn't swim too deep, where crickets hip-hopped in entertaining ways and didn't succumb too soon, and where there was always a warm home with a soft bed, and the security of knowing that cat baths had been outlawed from now until eternity's end.

The attack of the killer "Doberman" was still fresh in the minds of the inhabitants, although with the passing of each month, its gruesome details were recounted more as a mythical fairy tale than a real event that had nearly done away with them all. The true story was of such epic proportions that the living-memory version—amplified and glorified as these often are—became even more surreal in its verbal reenactment.

Fuzzy the Great was slowly being transformed in the minds of his subjects into a powerful warrior cat god that could slay the dog beasts with a sword that shot out deadly heart-piercing lightening bolts and a shield forged so strong that even the longest and sharpest venom-seething dog fangs could not hope to penetrate.

He was a legend in his own time, a true leader of leaders, a protector of the weak, defender of the innocent, keeper of the Holy Fish Mote, a walking representative and living image of everything that was good, moral, honest, and ethical.

Fuzzy the Great didn't wander out of his castle very much since like all the historically renowned cat leaders before him, he was a humble chap who didn't wish to draw more attention to himself or to be constantly showered with praise and adulation by the crowds that would quickly form when he took a stroll through any part of the Kingdom.

Thus, he spent a great deal of his waking hours stretched out on his favorite sofa in philosophical meditation, contemplating the evolution and development of the dominant species "feline" and how lucky they were to have a tranquil home where all could live in happiness and harmony.

Winter was quickly turning into spring—all the cats *knew* that *springtime* was coming (!)—and as you might imagine, the activity level of the Feline Kingdom was suddenly and pleasantly accelerated, especially in the wee hours of the morning. Yes, life was very, very good. And life was sort of more fun at the moment, too!

As snow gave way to green grass and blooming flowers, and freezing winds were overtaken by soft warm breezes, all of the cats began to rejoice with the knowledge that long days of lazing about in the meadows and valleys would soon be upon them. These would be the most luxuriously restful days of the whole year and everyone was making hasty preparations to take full advantage of each wonderful moment.

In the midst of all this physical and mental celebration, Scotty the Scout cat suddenly returned one day from his look-out post in the far reaches of the Feline Kingdom. He arrived worn and tired, out of breath from having run for long distances without stopping to rest or properly nourish himself. His degraded and distraught appearance attracted quite a lot of attention and by the time he arrived at Morty the Mayor's house, he had a large group of felines anxiously and curiously trailing behind him.

Scotty banged impatiently at the mayor's door, and after a few moments, Morty appeared and greeted the respected scout with open paws. "So good to see you, Scotty! You're looking a little under the weather—have you been feeling okay? Actually I thought your turn wasn't up in the outpost for another month or two, but it's good of you to pay us a visit anyway as I know it can get rather lonely out there all by oneself, especially during those cold, long winter months when..."

"Mr. Mayor! Thank you so much for your kind comments and your very nice greeting, but I have not come back because my turn is over nor am I here for a social visit, although I would have it that either one of those situations were true."

"Then why stand you here?", the mayor inquired with a puzzled and somewhat troubled look on his face.

"I'm afraid I have some very serious and perhaps even terrible news to report, sir," replied Scotty. "Let me get right to the point, considering the urgency of this situation. About three weeks ago, I was paid a visit from a fellow scout of another lesser Kingdom that lies quite some distance beyond the limits of our own sacred marked territories. He arrived at my outpost in an injured state and died shortly after having recounted his dramatic story."

"And what be this story?",insisted the mayor, as a huge crowd was now gathering around Morty and Scotty so that all could hear the details of what had happened in the distant lands.

Scotty continued by saying, "It seems that his Kingdom had been furiously and savagely attacked and that he was one of the lucky few to escape, having been assigned to the outpost. Those that had remained and had not been immediately killed, had been enslaved to do the dirty work of their new masters, knowing that their days were counted too as these aggressors never left any survivors behind. All hope was gone for any kind of counter-attack or recuperation of their once strong and peaceful Kingdom. They had been completely and totally dominated—annihilated—by the invasion force!"

"And this was not the worst of it!", warned Scotty. "According to the account I received from this fellow scout, these savage beasts would surely not be satisfied with having captured the Kingdom in the distant lands, but would seek out *more* land and riches until perhaps someday they were in control of *all* feline territories and could dominate *all* cats in *all* parts. They were aggressively seeking to rule the world!"

This brought about an uproar among the large crowd of cats who had been listening to Scotty's frightening story and it took the mayor a few minutes to get everybody calmed down so that he could request more details yet. When the panic had subsided a bit and Morty could once again gain control of the conversation, he asked that Scotty please continue with what else he had learned.

"This is the *worst* part, Mr. Mayor. Somehow, they learned of the feats of Fuzzy the Great, and in their feelings of superiority and triumph in having just conquered that other Kingdom, they began to mock Fuzzy the Great's abilities and skills. The more they talked and learned about his epic battle with the "Doberman," the more they disbelieved the tale and the more they wanted to confront Fuzzy the Great himself."

"Thus, it appears they have organized a war march towards our

Feline Kingdom with the expressed goal of making a fool of Fuzzy the Great and dominating and destroying the Kingdom he represents. With ambition and determination, and considering the favorable change of weather for ground travel, they could possible reach the outer limits of our Feline Kingdom within two weeks and be amongst us here another short two weeks thereafter. For that very reason, I have made such an effort to arrive here with all of you in the shortest possible time so that you may be forewarned of the danger that lurks about us."

The cat crowd went absolutely crazy upon hearing these last words and a panic shot through every nook and cranny of the once peaceful town. Many went running off to recount the tale to their friends and family; others remained at the mayor's house talking anxiously among themselves.

The mayor, very disconcerted but still with a self-controlled look upon his face—as is appropriate for anyone with a leadership kind of position—shouted out to the crowd demanding silence and quickly obtained his wish.

"There is just one more thing we must know. Who are these invaders? Who are these foul souls that so willingly threaten our lives, our very existence? Who must we soon face here in mortal combat in our peace-loving Feline Kingdom?"

Scotty turned pale and obviously didn't want to have to answer that question, but upon the continued insistence of the mayor, finally offered the following terrifying description.

"Well, sir, they're being called the 'Avenging Horde of Chihuahuas'. They're truly *savage* dog beasts, Mr. Mayor! I've been told that they're small and agile, with terrible shrieking, high-pitched barks that send a chill of fear right down your spine. They come in full body armor, with those nasty, pointy metal helmets strapped down tightly under their chins, which—when in a full run with head down—they can ram the tip through an innocent feline as if he were a shiskabob. And the worst thing of all, sir—there are *thousands* of them! They attack in wining, screaming Hordes and know no fear!"

With that, Scotty fainted and fell to the ground. His physical condition was so weakened and that, with the stress of having to relay this dramatic story, simply overwhelmed him and wouldn't allow him to continue on any more.

The Feline Kingdom was in a state of disarray. It was a sad day to be remembered forever in cat history.

How do I feel?

Chapter Three

"Dog face!" Yeah, I heard her call him that. Right out in the street, on the sidewalk, in front of my house, a young human couple was having some kind of heated argument, and suddenly, she called him, "*Dog* face!"

Think about it. If you were really ready to lay the verbal abusive punishment on someone, would you ever in your life shout out at the top of your lungs, "Hey, *cat* face!"

No, I don't think so. I mean, getting into someone's business and identifying them as "*dog* face" could bring you some serious trouble, but "*cat* face" would probably do no more than raise a few eyebrows and leave the "offended" wondering if he's really been offended at all.

Am I making a point here? Okay, I'll give you another chance, just in case. What if I say, "Wow, either we're living next to the city dump, or every time you even slightly exhale, you would make even the worst *dog breath* smell like a scented breeze from the magnolia trees in spring!"

Or what about making reference to your "floppy *dog ears*"? Or how about commenting on your "scraggly, tangled *doggy hair*"? Does that give you a good feeling? Would "that sneezing, dripping *dog snout*" get a rise out of you?

The deal is, when humans wanna be bad, and be bad verbally, it seems a whole lot of negative imagery can be generated in a big hurry just by slipping in the derisive and disgusting word "dog." Does that *really* surprise you? From my perspective at least, I see all this as the most natural, and in fact, logical kind of thing in the world. After all, we're talking about *dogs* here!

On the other hand, picture a "cat" in your head. Wow, it's just pure visual delight, isn't it! From head to tail, paw to well-formed paw, bright glow-in-the-dark eyes to soft beautiful fur—you name it, we're talking about the raw material that gods and goddesses are modeled from!

I don't want to brag or anything, but the facts are the facts and we might as well set them straight right from the beginning so there's no doubt left in anyone's mind about who's the superiorly cool species around these parts.

I suppose all this oughta make me feel really good, but the truth of the matter is—I don't feel the slightest thing at all. I mean, what's to get emotional about here? Like I said, "facts are facts" and we're just honing in a little on reality at the moment.

If cats are naturally sleek, swift, elegant, intelligent, alert, cuddly, affectionate, and loving—and dogs would be most easily and accurately described by the exact opposites of all that—then what's to feel "good" or "bad" about, huh? It's sort of like the luck of the draw, and you just gotta play out this hand with what you've been dealt. Is that so complicated? And don't worry—it's just *one hand*. The trick is to not lose sight of the *game* at large.

Humans, as you might already know, seem to make a big deal out of this "feeling" thing. I mean, a BIG deal. There's almost like a constant conscious and/or unconscious self- and external monitoring going on. This gives them continuous updates on the emotional feel-good/feel-bad level of themselves and their immediate environment. "Unplugging" them from this right hemispherical roller coaster could quite readily result in psychological chaos. At the very least, it would leave a void screaming out to be filled as soon as possible.

As a point of example, one of the problems I've personally experienced with the "owners" is knowing exactly how much affection to show and when to show it. This is tricky business, I'll tell you right up front, and especially for a species that is so naturally affectionate and loving like we cats.

To give you an idea about what I mean, I've learned that "affection" and "man owners" just don't mix when there's some kind—maybe even *any* kind—of sports program on the television. I can go into my super-duper leg circling, body rubbing, slippery sliding, high-volume purring walk and—nothing! At that moment, I'm a ghost, a non-entity, invisible to the world.

It shook me up a little the first few times it happened and I had to go running into the bedroom where they have that devious wall mirror thing to see if I were really still there or not. I finally came to learn that if you see a bunch of human guys on the screen getting real sweaty and bad-smelling (imagine the scent of any dog in your mind), that this meant there was going to be no "Fuzzy quality time" until some kind of definitive conclusion was reached as to which group had thoroughly out-sweated and out-grunted the other. This "finale" would bring about a clear look of extreme satisfaction or genuine disappointment on the face of the "man owner," depending on which clan he had emotionally joined forces with during the event.

If he, by some stroke of luck, ended up on the winning team, then that was my cue to go for broke. This could lead to some serious lap-sitting combined with back-stroking, string playing—even the breaking out of the delectable "kitty treats" on very, very good days. Nummmm!

On the other hand, if the "man owner's" team lost, the house would be swiftly transformed into a funeral-like atmosphere where the mourning of unrealized opportunities under adverse conditions had to be observed and respected by all who crossed his dreary and disheartened path. No, this was not a cat's ideal moment to hang out with the humans. Anyhow, I may get back to some of this entertainment kind of stuff later on.

You know, I mentioned the bedroom wall mirror a little while back, and that got me thinking about my first experience with that inanimate master of illusions. Those can be really frightening things, don't you think? I mean, they just hang out somewhere—all innocent looking—waiting to lure you in to their own little visually captive world where they can take control of your very soul if you aren't careful!

I've seen the "lady owner" walk into the bedroom in a good mood, come to a dead-stop in front of that mystifying silvery plane, mutter something about a "bad hair day," and just change her whole sense of well-being in a flash.

I was trying to figure this one out for a long time. It seems that "how I look" has some kind of direct connection with "how I feel," and that the devious mirror serves as a type of "spiritual medium" that brings the two elements together. I told you, it's scary, so watch out!

I clearly remember *my* first encounter with this mind-distorting demon a few years ago. I was just a kitty—cute, bubbling, and bouncing as you are surely imagining—when I casually strolled past the mirror's ever-present gaze one day. I glanced out of the corner of my eye and suddenly saw another kitty walking alongside me. As I looked even closer, I soon realized that this "mime beast" was exactly imitating my every move!

A state of shock and horror ran through my body. I stopped, in a crouched alert position, and it stopped, in a crouched alert position. I spun around, hissed, and struck at it with my right-front paw. Unfazed by my obvious ferocity, it spun around, hissed, and had the nerve to strike back at me—doing all this in what seemed to be simultaneous motion!

This last aggressive and uncalled for move on his part automatically activated the extremely agile spring mechanisms in all four of my legs, and shot me straight up in the air with one of us cat's famous fur out, tail up, fangs glaring, high-jump routines. If the Olympic Committee had seen me at that moment... Anyway, this twin kitty from the ether world had the nerve and the gall to do exactly the same thing once again!

This sent me off scrambling under the bed and I just stayed there, heart a racing, totally spooked out, until I was subsequently lured out several hours later by the "owners" with the sound of the can opener liberating some of those little cut-up fish. If it hadn't been for that, I might still be under that bed today, just wasting away, wondering how to get past that other kitty who had come uninvited and unannounced into my house!

Later on in life, I of course figured out that this reflective thing was really just some kind of super-advanced electronic photographic device that had been brought by aliens from another planet to permanently wreak havoc with the humans' minds and egotistical tendencies. You see, there's really not *another cat* in the mirror, but a tricky projection, at least in my case, of the perfect specimen of the feline species. I concluded that this was a way for the aliens to capture images of divine models from which they could go about improving their own distorted figures through sophisticated genetic alteration techniques, hoping one day to be more "Fuzzy-like," at least in their physical aspect. Fat chance, right!

The humans apparently haven't yet arrived at my advanced-level of understanding of the so-called "mirrors," so they just go bonkers when they get trapped in front of one of those things. They'll twist and twitch, spin around, make strange faces, do acrobatic poses, and then just walk off with that—"Oh well, I did the best I could!"—kind of look.

This all makes me think again of the "hair problem" regularly identified by the "lady owner" in one of those mirrors. My only possible thought here is that there must be some kind of "feeling sensors" imbedded in human hair that directly spark the emotional part of the brain, because if "the hair ain't right, then the best mood in the world just goes right down the drain."

The problem is, I've heard hair can be "unruly." At least that's what they say. What does that mean? They must want to "rule" hair then, to dominate it, to be its master, to govern it, to lord over it, to feel that *their* wish is *its* command.

But, hair has a mind of its own. It will not so easily be submitted to the whims of the human carrying it around. It can be a rebel without a cause, or without a "look," as the case may be. It can foil the best laid plans for psychological tranquillity and might, when teamed with its partner-in-crime "wind," do incredible flying tricks that would make even the best of the humans want to don a full hood and wander anonymously in the high mountains among the Tibetan Monks.

The head is the chariot of hair. They are inseparable, bonded into a "oneness" that makes their behavior, appearance, and appreciation mutually dependent. And in the head, are stored up all those emotions that humans have to deal with. Maybe that's why hair is such a big deal, huh? It sort of puts a decorative lid on all those feel-good, feel-bad things, and even when a human has had really a lousy day, if his hair passes the muster, well, look out world!

I've heard through listening in on conversations that one of the most traumatic experiences of all can be the thing called the "haircut." Have you ever in your life seen a cat get one of those? We're much more sensible than the humans in that as kitties, we grow out the fur to the appropriate length and styling, and then just keep it that way the rest of our days. No big thing there. Do it once, do it right, and then leave it alone!

Some *dogs* I've known get these wimpy-looking designer cuts from some mutt parlor where they come back temporarily smelling like an overgrown flower bed, and unbelievably, might even have their nails clipped in the process too! Like what are they thinking? "Oh my gosh, if Rover next door sees me with these long nails, I'll just die of embarrassment!"

They strut around thinking they've been physically pampered into some higher life form, not realizing all the time that they look like some ridiculous goon that just got off a spaceship from the planet Irksome. I even saw this ribbon pegged on top of this recently groomed and clipped mutt's head once and she was prancing around as if she were God's gift to the utterly prissy. I couldn't look at wrapped birthday presents without becoming sick to my stomach for at least two years after that sight for sore eyes!

And what's this hormone growth thing you humans have got going on anyway? You're just never satisfied—when it comes to hair, it's grow, grow, grow, grow. Lighten up, eh! And then those that can't grow it anymore just let it fall off like a crew abandoning its ship. Remember, you gotta put a lid on the kettle or the contents are just gonna boil over one day. You just don't want the lid changing sizes all the time either.

It's one extreme to the other. Look, you've got us cats around, fortunately, as role models in this area and you can see that we look just great *all the time* with absolutely no stressing out on this hair/fur thing. Pay attention, and you might learn something!

Getting back to the "haircut experience," I've seen humans nearly go into comatose shock when they call to make an appointment with their stylist and are told that, "I'm sorry, but she no longer works here." This is almost the equivalent of hearing, "I'm sorry, but all life on earth will end at midnight tonight."

They go into a panic. "What? What do you mean? Did she *die* or just go to another place to work? You *don't know* where she's working now! You *must* know, but you just don't want to tell me. Look, I'll give you my house, my new car, and my first born if you just give me a clue as to her whereabouts. You've gotta know something! She's the *only one* in the universe who knows exactly how I like my hair cut, and she has even learned to deal with that difficult area in the back that nobody else knows about. You've gotta *help* me! Please, don't leave me all alone and abandoned in this cold, cruel world like this!"

And so it goes. Finally, the realization sets in that they're going to have to put their hair under the guidance of someone "new." "New"—meaning, inexperienced with *my hair*, a novice, a butcher, a slayer of "the look" that I've so carefully developed over the decades. A shaky-handed and unfeeling assassin with a dull pair of rusty scissors wearing cracked and smudged tri-focals an inch thick!

"Okay," they say, "then give me an appointment at 3:00 p.m. with the new stylist dungeon master because I've got a big meeting tomorrow and I have to do *something*. By the way, what's her name? *Grunilda*! But, what? Everyone calls her '*Snippy*'!"

They arrive at the stylist place in a full sweat with a hyper-anxiety equivalent to a mouse who's just been told that "Fuzzy's been seen around these parts lately." (And you better believe, that's some serious anxiety!) They sit down in the waiting area, cross their legs, uncross their legs, cross them again, all the time trying to figure out something to do with their hands, which are going completely out of control at the moment.

Fortunately, the ubiquitous magazine rack is spotted, where one can always find a huge collection of four-year-old editions with tattered covers and smudged pictures. They grab a copy, *any* copy, and begin to devour every word of every story with a passion—even though their job profession and personal interests are in the financial markets and this particular magazine is a special on the preparation and cultivation of indoor potted plants. No matter, because this completely takes their mind off the soon-to-be kami-kazi "test run" of the virgin stylist.

Just when the stomach cramps are starting to subside and the sweat stops pouring down the back of their neck, the dreaded moment comes as their name is being called to approach "the chair." They enter with a crooked smile pasted on their face, trying to put on an air of self-confidence, thinking that this might put a little caution in the trembling, swollen hands of Snippy before she begins to think about mutilating what they've worked years to achieve.

They sit down slowly, eyeing all the various cutting instruments displayed around them, wondering if, as in their wildest dreams, Snippy might by some chance skillfully and adeptly use each one of them, changing from one to the other like a seasoned surgeon in the world's best and most renowned medical clinic.

They also wonder if, as in their wildest nightmares, she might just grab the first thing she can get her grubby little hands on—a semi-broken small pair of scissors used by her obnoxious daughter for cutting pictures out of magazines—and proceed to lash at their once-perfect hairstyle all the way through until only a bleeding scalp and a few patches of uneven strands remained.

Well, Snippy tucks them under the proverbial haircutting garb—used to prevent any fast escapes—and then comes out with the standard, "So what can we do for you today?" Yes, that was the *perfect* question, because it allows them to go into a forty-minute verbal dissertation on the history and sequential development of the particular hair style arrived at today. This is accompanied by the viewing of a very thick photo album they have brought with them, so that Snippy could also have the chance to physically study their hair trend as it had progressed over the years—with regular interjections on little details of how their old faithful, now missing stylist had handled certain aspects around the ears or on the neckline.

About two hours later—for a five-minute trim—they walk out of the stylist shop looking just the same as usual and feeling pretty good about themselves for having so expertly managed and trained this *new*, novice stylist. These shops have these *mirror* things all over the place—obviously an alien focal point for earth R&D—so they had the chance to get repeated looks at all sides of their head and took care to get every hair in its proper cut and location before giving her the "go ahead" for the concluding non-threatening blow dry. Feeling good about the whole experience, they could now comfortably cross out the old stylist's name in their address book and fill in "Snippy" under "H" for hair.

This makes me think—isn't it funny what makes humans "feel good"? I may never figure this one completely out. The best I can do is to compare these "emotional states" with a roller coaster I once saw at Disney World. It's a lot of "ups" and "downs"—usually changing quickly and when they least expect it—that just keeps them on edge all the time.

Actually, us cats can be quite sensitive beings too. Notice that I said "sensitive," not "emotional." There's a difference. "Sensitive" is like when one of the "owners" yells at me for no good reason, just because he's in a bad mood. I may not always show it, but it hurts me inside and can give me that wide-eyed kind of shivering throughout my whole body. It's a sub-conscious kind of thing that goes right to the very soul sometimes, but usually can't be expressed very well in words.

"Emotions," on the other hand, are more violent, disruptive, *volatile* types of reactions that humans say come from the heart, but really are more head-related and depend a whole lot on how they let their external environment impact on them. These things are really less important in the run of things, yet I see can be very dramatic and unpredictable in their effects.

It's like one day a lot money makes them happy and the next day it's meaningless. At one moment their relationship with a certain person is the key in their life, and the next moment it's just of secondary importance. Something "fishy" is going on here, I do believe.

"Sensitivity" is *real* because it has the same impact whenever, whereas "emotions" seem at least somewhat false in that there's just too much "roller coaster" in them, if you know what I mean. The problem is, humans "*make* them real." They begin to worry, analyze, theorize, conceptualize, explain, justify, and all that. Why don't they just leave it alone?

Us cats aren't emotional—we just "are." "Sensitive," yes, because things will make us happy or sad, angry or tranquil—but these "things" make their impact without interpretation or justification. They just do it. This is what is *really* meant by "feeling from the heart." It's pure reaction, and nothing more. You gotta keep the head out of it or you get going on those "ups" and "downs" we talked about. And those will do your stomach and everything else in with it.

There you have it—"real" versus Disney World. Disney World is great. It's just that it's a nice place to visit, but you can't live there. My experience with humans has shown me though that most of them do live in their own little amusement park. Actually, I shouldn't say "little," because normally it's this super elaborate affair that has been very well developed and constructed over the years.

That's why I like to hang out with little human babies sometimes—we're more in tune with each other. They cry when they want to eat, smile and giggle when they're happy, but there's really no *thinking* involved. They're just *reacting* naturally to their environment and their feelings. They're *sensitive* creatures. Babies are *real* people. We cats are for real. I hate to admit it, but even the disgusting canines of the world are real. So what happened to humans, in general? How do they *feel*?

Okay, now *I'm* analyzing too much. Whenever that happens, the best thing to do is nod off for a few winks. Maybe a *whole bunch* of winks. Sounds like the purrfect idea!

Morty the Mayor, now having a complete understanding of the very serious threat to their existence that would soon come from the Avenging Horde of Chihuahuas, knew he had to take action immediately. And there was *one* and *only one* course of action to be considered. Fuzzy the Great must be consulted on this matter!

Morty went walking in a dignified fashion toward Fuzzy the

Great's castle, which lie on the outskirts of the Feline Kingdom. He was being careful to retain a proper mayoral image and also, not scare his cat citizens even more by heading off in a full run as was his first inclination. He arrived at the fish mote surrounding the castle in about 15 minutes, with a huge group of citizenry trailing anxiously behind him.

The draw bridge had been left down—actually it was always left in that position since the Kingdom had been at peace from the time of the defeat of the "Doberman"—so he strolled up to the huge wooden doors and pounded three times with the round metal knockers. There was no answer, so he let the clanging resound throughout the castle three more times, and waited patiently at the entrance.

Fuzzy the Great was in his huge and well-equipped earthen-stone kitchen at the time, with a wooden fire burning brightly and hotly in the big iron stove. He was about to cut up into small pieces one of the fish he had gotten from his mote that morning so as to enjoy a fried delicacy that would delight even the most distinguished feline taste buds. At that moment, he heard the rapping at his doors.

He slowly walked through the long, dimly lit corridors of his castle—there was never any reason to hurry these days—and with the creaking, squeaking sound of huge, heavy wooden planks securely fastened on sturdy, old and rusting iron hinges, opened his abode to face a crowd of almost all the catfolk of the Kingdom. The mayor was standing alone, in front, with a most serious look on his tired, old face.

Morty broke the silence by extending the typical greeting one would give to a mythological cat warrior god, praising him for past conquests and feats, and wishing him much health and a long life.

After quite some time—in part distracted by having been taken away from his half-prepared fish and in part rather shocked by the huge turnout at his front door—Fuzzy the Great returned a short and appropriate greeting to the mayor and then to all others gathered in his sight.

With the formalities taken care of, Morty the Mayor got right to the point. He recounted the story that Scotty the Scout had told them, not leaving out even the most minor detail. It was important that Fuzzy the Great be fully informed so as to be able to evaluate the true urgency of the situation and the possible recourses they may have to respond.

Fuzzy the Great made no movements nor showed even the slightest emotion all the time the mayor was talking, but he was carefully taking mental notes of every bit and piece of information divulged. Having finished his story, Morty and the crowd stood like statues, in a frozen silence, awaiting the response of their true warrior leader.

"Action must be taken, and it must be taken immediately. We cannot waste a moment's time in our preparation for what is sure to be a savage and brutal attack of this wining Horde you so adeptly have described. We..."

The tension had become so great in the crowd that even though it was rude to do so in front of their warrior god, the cats of the Kingdom began to shout out their feelings and ideas in a nervous, rapid, and uncontrolled fashion.

"It's not fair. It's just not fair! Why must they attack *us*? We have lived in peace and mean harm to no being."

"I say we give them what they're asking for! We can also prepare full body armor and craft little pointy helmets and meet them on their own terms. Let's give them..."

"There's no time for that! The forging of such weaponry would take us *months*, and they will be at the outer limits of our marked territories in perhaps just *two week's time*!"

"I agree. We need a plan that is both *strong* and *fast*. If we do not prepare ourselves well and quickly, we will surely all perish under the grip of their sharpened fangs."

"But there are *thousands* of them and they are battle-ready and blood-thirsty! We are a peaceful lot having spent years now in a non-violent environment, not having practiced or refined what should be our naturally strong fighting skills. Considering our weakened state of preparation, I insist that we send a representative committee to meet them on their march and negotiate a mutually agreeable resolution. I'm sure they will see our point of..."

"You speak the words of a *coward* and a *crazy cat*! I would rather die in battle defending my home than to negotiate with those wining, snapping little canine beasts! I still have most of my claws even at my age and I will surge into their ranks with no fear and strike down as many of those Chihuahua devils as I can before they take away my final breath!"

"Those are the words of a *true warrior* and I will join you, fighting side by side, tooth for nail, and we shall diminish their ranks you and I, in a grand flurry of fur and..."

And so on they went, for almost two hours, shouting out idea after idea until finally they had run the gamut of options and emotions and the catfolk once again returned to their silent, statue-like state. All this time, Fuzzy the Great stood respectfully by, listening attentively and without emotion to all comments made. This was the sign of a truly great leader, and all knew and recognized this, as he would hear out and take into consideration any and all ideas. But in the end, *he* and *only he*, would make the final judgment as to what should be done. This final judgment would be accepted and respected without question, as this was how things had always been done and always would be done in the Feline Kingdom.

Fuzzy the Great disappeared into his castle, returning a few minutes later with his famous sword in one paw and his shield in the other. This tremendously impressive image was received by a clamorous, long round of applause and heightened positive emotional energy by all present. He stood there, chest puffed out, and with his most powerful and domineering voice, began his discourse.

"Fellow and respected catfolk of the Feline Kingdom. I have listened to you speak and I have taken into consideration each and every idea expressed this crucial day. You have expressed proud words of bravery, and genuine fears. You have stated your concerns, and your hopes. You have formulated plans of attack, and scenarios for defense. And through all of this you have given me vision and inspired me with confidence!"

"Confidence in *you* as a good and caring citizenry, who when called upon in times of need, will come together as *one* and find superior and amplified strength in this unity."

"Confidence in the *Feline Kingdom* to rise up and meet this hideous, pointy-helmeted, squeaking, wining, short-legged vermin."

"Confidence in *myself*, as your leader, to take our abilities to a level they have never gone before nor have ever had to go before."

"From your strength of emotions and power of expression, you have fired me with the will and resolve to lead you once again on this new and urgent challenge thrust upon us!"

A huge and noisy round of applause erupted from the crowd, and Fuzzy the Great continued on in great fashion.

"To not only throw back, but to resoundly defeat once and for all this Horde of midget menaces, we must draw up the most creative of all creative plans."

"We must be *sly*, slyer than the mountain streams that carve their way through thick, hard surfaces to aptly reach their desired destinations far, far below the summit."

"We must be *crafty*, craftier than the whispering winds that tunnel their way through the dark, dank forests to find their airy freedom in the open plains that lie beyond."

"We must be *swift*, swifter than the teams of huge, fluffy clouds that navigate their awkward pillowly bodies through the strong and unpredictable currents of air to allow them to release their live-giving sustenance in the anointed locations."

"My friends, my fellow citizens of the Feline Kingdom, above all, we must be cats, drawing upon every inherited and evolved element of our proud feline ancestry to help us arch our backs high, raise our tails tall, and spring our claws forth in unnerving defiance! As proud and brave cat warriors, there is no challenge we cannot meet, no enemy we cannot conquer!"

As Fuzzy the Great paused a bit to catch his breath, a tremendous and even noisier and longer round of applause broke out. This lasted perhaps fifteen minutes, with a chanting and syncopated clapping that carried the exuberant sounds echoing far out of the Kingdom and into the woods that lie beyond.

They shouted, "Fuzzy, Fuzzy, Fuzzy, Fuzzy..." and though it arrived in a muted and whispering form, the front lines of the swiftly advancing Horde of Avenging Chihuahuas got a good earful of this distant and jubilant celebration.

Upon hearing the strong chanting of the name of their next targeted enemy carried over the land by the resonating winds, the Horde suddenly stopped its advancement and went into a swerving, circling, snarling frenzy. It was like a spark that set off a gigantic bonfire of violent emotions that brought the dust up from the earth below them into a huge, twisting tornado of rage.

All at once, rising up tall and strong from amongst the middle of these thousands of growling, snapping little warrior beasts, was the leader of the Horde. He was a *huge* canine known as Chucky the Chihuahua, perhaps twice the size of any other in his Horde or any other of his breed that had ever set paws on earth. With an acidic saliva dripping from his long, blood-stained fangs and his chest fully puffed out beneath the glimmering silver body armor, he ferociously growled for silence so that he could speak.

"You have heard what I have heard, gurrrrrrrrrr, and this has made your blood boil with the hate of the feline scourge that lies ahead. We, gurrrrrrrrrr, know now that we march not in vain, but that we are about to embark on a glorious mission to rid, gurrrrrrrrrr, once and for all, these fertile lands of these independent-minded and self-confident, tree-climbing wimps called 'cats.' And we hear the name of, gurrrrrrrrrr, 'Fuzzy' being echoed throughout the land, which alerts us to the fact that our most sought after of all enemies awaits our arrival."

"And *arrive we shall*! With shields in close, swords to the front, and heads up high, we shall strike with such a swift and deadly force that the Feline Kingdom will submit to our dominance in a matter of minutes, running about with their tails between their legs and their broken, false sense of courage lying shattered on the ground beneath them. And, gurrrrrrrrrr, the Feline Kingdom shall be *ours*!

Ours, , gurrrrrrrrrr, ours, , gurrrrrrrrrr, ours, , gurrrrrrrrrr, ours..."

The chanting continued amidst the revival of the growling, whirling frenzy, which, this time, was carried back on the winds toward the Feline Kingdom. The violent sounds of terror soon permeated the sensitive ears of each and every cat and brought about a deadly silence like no other before. Fuzzy the Great, unfazed and unshaken by all this, spoke once again.

"I have a plan. A *grand plan*. But, for this to be successful, we must work *together*. We must *join forces* as a team."

"You know that we are a *superior* species. You know that we are swifter, stronger, and more intelligent. You know that we are more cunning, agile, and come equipped with sharper and faster claws."

"But they are many, and we are few. They are stupid and violent, which can be very dangerous in large numbers. They are ruled by emotion at this moment, which can be very deadly when set off in a heightened and negative form. And worst of all, they are *avenging*, which can be a most blinding and powerful force in battle."

"For that reason, we must seek out special means to confront and conquer the Chihuahua. To do so, we shall construct a very special wartime device that I have conceived of, called the "Chidozer." This will surely give us that little edge needed to not only stop the assault of our enemy, but to rid the Feline Kingdom and all cats' lands of them once and for all. Fear not, my friends and fellow citizens, for we shall come out victorious!"

How smart is smart?

Chapter Four

Today was going to be a great day! A day of days, a day for all times, a day to be remembered, a day like no other. And what was bringing about all this joyous anticipation of the forthcoming hours? It was simple—Snowball was coming over to visit!

If you don't know who Snowball is, she's sort of like my girl..., well, a friend, who is a girl, who hangs out with me sometimes. We always have a fantastic time together. She's a beautiful, smaller, delicate, soft-furred, all white feline that'll get your motor going even on the coldest of nights!

"Motor"—yeah—it's the thing the humans call "purring," I believe. A very interesting concept indeed, this purring. You see, we've got this little self-activating motor deep, down inside the very essence of our bodies—located in the sensitivity cavity of the frontal vibration chamber, if I recall correctly from my earlier cat physiology studies. It's preset at the factory to go off automatically at specified times—usually by things like a good bit of genuine attention displayed to us by a human; a satisfying meal of little cut-up fish; a soft, safe little napping area accompanied by a long, licking bath; or just any kind of pleasant activity or thought that should happen to come along.

Once the motor gets a humming, it may go on for a *very* long time and even come with sound effects on very special occasions.

That's the real epitome of the feel-good, sound-good kind of thing. It just makes ya warm and happy all over!

Well, that's how I was feeling this morning because it was going to be great day! A day of days, a day for all—I think I'm rambling here. Did I tell you Snowball was coming over?

She strolled up the front yard about mid-morning, looking as elegant and well-groomed as ever, and took her usual curving, twisting, round-about way up to the porch where I was stretched out real long-like on the top step. I'll fill you in that this sort of impresses the female felines if you don't look overly excited about their arrival and give that big, tough-cat image all the while.

We were already sending off tons of non-verbal signals that even the smartest human wouldn't have caught sight of, but oh well, what can I say? It's just their normal kind of preoccupation with their own little world and the emphasis on all those *words*.

For example, why did I just remain lying there? Another cat was obviously invading my marked territory and this would normally call for a swift and sometimes violent response. My non-action in this case clearly indicated that a "welcome intrusion" was taking place; in other words, that we already knew each other and that she was expected. See how it works?

What about her entrance? Why all the curving, twisting action? In this case, "welcome" or not, one just can't enter like a speeding bullet toward the host! The fact remains that this is still the private territory of *Fuzzy*, under his full domain and control. The slow, swerving approach communicates quite clearly that the guest recognizes her special privilege of treading on another's land. She thus humbles herself before him through her body language, in respect for his governance. That's really not so complicated, is it?

I've gotta ask ya—what happened to the non-verbal element in humans? Actually, I see them using it all the time—certain movements of the head, eyes, mouth, arms, hands; postures they take in standing, walking, and sitting; the speed of their respiration; the aura of colors they emit; and so on. They're experts, really. The only thing is, I get the feeling they're only slightly aware of the huge quantity of subtle messages that are being transmitted, at least on a conscious level.

It's a shame, don't you think? All that power of expression built into the human communicative machine and so little perception or understanding. Just think of the possibilities if they only knew how to better recognize and use it for their own benefit.

We cats, on the other hand, have got this non-verbal thing down to a science. You just have to know what to look for—and then, *look for it*! Let's take the "tail" as an example. How about a *tale* about a *tail*? Sorry, that just sort of slipped out.

Marvelous creation, don't you think? It's a multi-use, multi-feature kind of device. It helps us balance ourselves when doing the "fence walk," it serves as a protective shield of certain vital elements when locked in battle, it communicates all kinds of feelings without an accompanying word, and perhaps best of all, it makes us look just really cool as we strut around with it waving from side to side.

Some dogs I've seen have their tails sawed off by some really barbarian and uncaring humans because I've heard that with their "breed," that's the way they're really supposed to look. What does that mean? If they were *born* with tails, then who in the world made the unmitigated judgment that all dogs of that breed just made a wrong turn in the evolutionary path and are mistakenly still created with tails on them? Does that make sense to you? Who has that kind of divine insight?

Personally, it gives me the willies seeing those poor mutilated mutts walking around like that. They try to do the "wagging" thing and there's just this little, lonely stump that isn't long enough to carry out the wagging or any of the other good things I just mentioned about tails in general.

Don't you see what they're really cutting off here—a part of the very *essence* of what it means to be a "dog"! Makes me really wonder about this superior-inferior thing sometimes, as I have the feeling I'm getting down far too hard on the canines.

Speaking of the "fence walk"...I was speaking of that, wasn't I? You know what I'm talking about. This is one of our more admired acrobatic feats that would get us onto any Olympic gymnastic team in the world if we were so inclined.

Take any narrow and even shaky, rickety fence—like those tall, thin wooden ones—and we can cross it. No problem! No, I don't mean *jump over* it, although that's easier yet, but *walk along the top* of it for long distances. Have you had the privilege of seeing one of these cat high-wire acts in person? It'll make you wish you'd been born with four legs and fur!

Nothing very tricky here really, as the key is to just *get into* what you're doing. You have to "be one" with the fence. The fence is you and you are the fence. If we did this in the Olympics, they'd probably call it the "karma fence" routine. Has a nice transcendental ring to it, doesn't it! "And the gold medal for the best karma goes to...who will not be required to reincarnate in the next competition four years from now!"

I think most humans attempting something like this would be so overwhelmed by the "fear" thing that they'd just crash to the ground in an embarrassing mess before they got the chance to take the first step. Gives me a rather funny and satisfying image when I imagine that in my head, you know.

Anyway, here's how it works in case you want to give it a try someday. First, you approach the fence, precisely estimating its height (for accurate jumping) and quality and age of construction (for proper balancing). Second, you hunch back real good so as to fully load the super spring action in your back legs. Third, in one swift and elegant movement, you land with all fours on top of the tall, wooden planks. (Don't leave out the "elegant" part because remember—you get judged on "style" as well as "ability".)

Fourth, spend a few moments adjusting your paws for their best gripping position and get your tail waving around to correct any problems of equilibrium. Fifth, begin to stroll down the planks, head held high (the "style" thing again) and move yourself along a minimum of half the distance of the total fence line so any admiring observers will know that you're fully under control of what you're doing and didn't just get lucky with a few meager steps.

Sixth, even though the awe-struck audience begs for more, go ahead and jump down and go about the rest of your business of the day because after all, there'll always be another cat, on another fence, another day, for those who really appreciate a show of perfect execution.

You can see how tails play a crucial role in the balancing act, but that's just the physical *end* of things. Did you catch that? Physical "end," like the *tail* is on the *end* of the...oh well. What about all the non-verbal stuff we were talking about? Believe it or not, tails are even more important in this aspect. I'll give you a few examples.

How about a cat who goes strolling through his house with his tail raised high? What does that communicate to you humans? It's easy, right? Happiness! We're just as happy as we can be when we point the ole thing up towards the heavens like a lightening rod.

It's like when I get to follow one of the "owners" around the house—preferably the "lady owner"—because she's a lot more talkative than the "man owner." That can be loads of fun for a cat because we like to have company once in a while and besides, I just sort of want to see what she's up to in her spare time.

I've found that a Saturday is usually the best chance to play the "follow-the-leader game" since she doesn't start up her go-to-work frenzy that day, which changes the whole daily routine. She usually gets herself busy in the morning with all kinds of strange tasks. One of my favorite things to watch is when she pulls this air-sucking thing out of the closet.

Strangest animal you've ever seen! It's got these little, round rolling feet that are no good for jumping or climbing or running very fast, and this long, skinny neck with no head on it! I've been postulating that its head might be hidden somewhere below because I see what I think are its eyes light up way down low close to the ground. Suppose that low-level head positioning is good for eating as it doesn't have to bend over to find its food down on the floor. I have at least been able to verify that the mouth definitely got situated in between the four little feet. Bet you think I'm making this all up, don't you?

It seems that it needs a little help walking, as the "lady owner" will grab ahold of it by the neck, pet it in some special area, and—you're not going to believe this—but it starts *purring* with the most *outrageous* sound I've ever heard from any animal in my life!

It's like I wanna be scared and run away, yet at the same time, it makes such a beautiful, harmonious purring noise that I just shoot my tail straight up in the air and go walking around behind the "lady owner"—a "safe" distance, of course, enjoying every fun-filled moment of this wonderful experience.

And can it *eat*! She goes leading it around all over the place and it just sucks up everything in sight—dead bugs I've left around for decorative purposes, little loose lint toys that I've pawed into submission, bits of paper here and there that I've carefully shredded. Not too picky, is it! That's a real *tail-raising* kind of happiness that I hope everyone has the chance to enjoy at some point in their lives.

Okay, a second non-verbal test. A cat quickly flicks the end part of his tail around many times from side-to-side, making it bang on the floor or things around it. You figured it out, didn't you? Yep, some*thing* or some*body* has got us ticked off!

You don't wanna make a cat mad. Really. It's like when the "man owner" sits down on his comfy chair—one of those strange, reclining things that when it opens up, creates a great secret hiding place underneath. I used to go zooming into the mysterious, dark cave of the chair when it exposed its secret entrance and just lie in there all secure and satisfied with myself—far away from any human's reach. But then, I discovered that if I didn't get out before the "man owner" decided to get up, it suddenly slammed the door shut, trapping me within its evil, wiry, dusty confines.

At first, I'd just sit there awhile trying to think of the secret password to get the thing to open itself up again, but after many failed attempts, I'd have to go into a low, howling meow so as to alert the "owners" of my predicament.

I'd hear them innocently say, "Is that *Fuzzy* meowing?" And I'd scream back, "*No*, it's not *Fuzzy* meowing! It's just this reclining, opening-closing *demon* piece of furniture you brought into my house that suddenly gained a life of its own and has begun to talk to you! *Get me out of here! Now!*"

They'll then walk around the place for what seems like hours—

trying to discover the source of my distress call—until they finally venture upon my synthetic, high-backed and well-armed captor.

"Oh, Fuzzy must be inside the *recliner*! What do you think he's doing in there?", They'll sarcastically remark.

"Well, to tell you the truth, I just thought I'd *asphyxiate myself* in this dark little hole because I had nothing better to do today! *Get me out of here! Right now!*"

Finally, they open up the secret door and I shoot out like a bullet, standing in front of them with fiery, glaring eyes and flicking my tail around like nobody's business. Being totally insensitive and ignorant of the non-verbal lashing I'm giving them at that moment, they find the whole situation sort of funny and begin to laugh, saying, "Oh Fuzzy, what a *silly* cat you are!"

"Silly? I nearly *died*! It was horrible! I was trapped. Penned in. Boxed up. Cornered. Held hostage. Cruelly and rudely denied my freedom of movement. Check out my *tail*, would ya! Can't you see this has put me in a *really foul mood*? Aren't you even looking?"

Nothing. Nope, I'm just a "big, amusing Fuzzy" to them—like I do life and death stunts for the humans' entertainment or something! You guys have really got to get your non-verbal act together—the sooner, the better.

One more chance, but this is your *last* one on the non-verbal tail communications. I'll give you something really easy, so you at least get *one* right. How about "tail between the legs"?

Unless you're totally tuned out at the moment, you must be thinking "fear," and when one thinks about fear, the first thing that obviously comes to mind is "doorbells." We talked about "purring," right? Well, this is the exact terrifying opposite—as sounds go.

Who invented doorbells anyway? It must have been some really sick, monstrous, *avenging* human. Avenging? Why does that word stir up strange memories of someone called "Chucky"? Maybe that's the guy who invented the doorbell. Chucky the Scientist. Chucky the Doorbell Man. Chucky the Experimenter. Chucky the Sound Creator. No, just doesn't ring a bell.

You see, the problem is with these things is that they go off when you least expect it. I don't know exactly where they live in the house or what makes them mad, but sure enough, I'll be all curled up in the middle of nice nap when it will suddenly go into a tantrum. I've heard there are different breeds that speak different languages, but I can tell you for sure that the one who got into my house communicates with a loud, low-tone, buzzing-screaming voice that will send terror-movie type chills right through your whole body until they ping pong off your very soul.

The first outburst from the doorbell beast always rockets my head up with such a speed that I nearly yank my whole vertebrae completely out of joint. Just when I'm starting to relax a little and I'm thinking it might have been part of a dream, the thing bellows out again! This fires me out of my soft, little cat bed into a full, upright, totally freaked out stance, wondering from which side or what distance the enemy invasion was coming from. With the third screaming rage, and absolutely no sign of my assayers anywhere in sight, my only recourse is to run like all get out—tail tucked safely between my legs—because you obviously can't defend yourself against what you can't see. It's really the *only* option.

That's probably the worst part of the whole thing—it's such a sly, tricky being that it never even shows its face when in attack mode. I figure it's some kind of genetically engineered *stealth animal* developed by the military for secret missions yet to be explained to the public at large. What else could it be?

Well, that was quite a tale of tails, wasn't it! Hope you got something out of that. I bet deep down it makes you at least a little bit jealous, if you were to be really honest with yourself, wishing you had a such a communicative body part that could express all those ideas without even opening your mouth. Luck of the draw, right? Us cats hit the *jackpot* on this one!

I don't want to make you feel bad or anything, but we've got more than just the *tail* going for us in the realm of sophisticated communication. Let's talk "talking," huh?

You guys call it "meowing" only because you've never bothered to learn our language, but we really get into our own deep, intellectual conversations when the mood strikes us. Since I don't have the time—or you, the patience—to go through our syntax and phonology, how about if I just give you a couple of *non-verbal* ways to interpret our "meows"? Better than nothing, right! I'll try to keep it simple.

First example: you hear sort of a rising-tone, high-pitched series of meows coming from your favorite cat. What's being communicated? Did you get it? It has to do with "getting your attention," right? Normally, we either "want *attention*" at that moment or "want *something else*." Check it out the next time.

The key is the word "want," and it's your job—if you've got any sensitivity in ya at all—to immediately and appropriately fully satisfy what we're after. That's the "nice" thing to do because we don't just go around asking for affection or other stuff all the time; and when we do, it means that you oughta pay attention and give us that little boost we're looking for.

It's like in the mornings when you humans are doing your kitchen routine. In my house at least, this routine always eventually involves freeing the sacred milk container from its chilly, suffocating prison. Out it comes, much to my continued and daily delight! I instantly go into the rising-tone, high-pitched series of meows—clearly alerting the "owners" that whenever they're ready, they can serve me a little of that precious, white delicacy too!

I remember at first that they just didn't catch on that I wanted to participate in the routine and partake of this heavenly drink-of-the-gods with them. They'd serve themselves a more-than-ample portion and then selfishly return the most sought-after container back to its prison cell. Humans can be so tuned out to what's going on around them sometimes, don't you think!

Well, after months of perseverance through careful repetitions on my part, they finally got the idea that I was regularly and energetically communicating my desire for "breakfast communion" with them, and that their total lack of cognizance of my needs had been frustrating the daylights out of me. They had been walking out of the kitchen belching satisfaction, and I was left with that empty, groaning feeling that comes from an ignored and hollow stomach!

Don't worry about it. Now they're completely trained and know what to do as far as the milk container goes, so everything has worked out okay. My next challenge in this area is to loosen them up on some of the other things that come out of that chilly chest, like cheese; meat—doesn't have to be cooked first...I'm not picky; yogurts—no fruit, please; eggs—uncooked, in this case; and other assorted and tempting goods. I've been trying my best, but they've been awfully stubborn with these items.

One more example of our cat language, and then we're changing subjects. How about those deep, slow, elongated meows that we do just once in a while? Any ideas? Well, it could be that we're "angry," but most often it's more like being "disturbed" or "upset" about something that has recently happened.

In this case, a little affection on your part wouldn't hurt, even though at times that may not take us out of the mood we're in right away. Give us a good, soft stroking anyway, eh, because a little affection never hurts anyone at any time of the day! What've ya got to lose?

This reminds me of the cats in the house next door. There's a *bunch* of them over there—I think about nine or ten. Their "owners" must have to bring in the little round cans by the truckload to keep all them happy!

Well, the oldest one is a big, shiny, short-haired black male who of course, for reasons of seniority, is in charge of the group. He and I don't talk much because of the adjoining territory thing that requires us to carefully mark out the boundaries and then keep our distance a little. Actually, I think he's a pretty good cat, but for "appearance" reasons, we stay on our own side of the line and thus maintain our semblance of control and respect in front of the others. It's a cat thing you wouldn't fully understand.

I had to go over to their place once—actually *enter* the house—because my "owners" sometimes hang out with their "owners." You see, my "man owner" picked me up in his arms and before I knew what was going on or had time to react, he was carrying me into the neighbor's yard, up their steps, and—after a short and unexpected attack by another doorbell beast—into their dwelling. This was clearly an open violation of territorial rights on my part, even though I had been forced to do it in hostage form.

As I was so rudely transported into the foreign abode, a curious and rather hostile-looking crowd of felines quickly gathered around the living room—all eyes fixed on me. The "man owner" just plopped me down on their couch and said, "Okay, Fuzzy, go off and play with your little friends!"

"You've gotta be kidding!", I blurted out, as I hunched way down in the cushion, tail under, ears back, waiting any moment for a full-scale, all-sides assault. I guess by sheer luck that day, all the humans quickly got involved in a conversation and completely forgot about me, leaving me in my original motionless, heart-racing position until it was time to go home. I think that was the longest hour and a half in my life!

As I was lying there, I had the chance to observe what was going on around me. After about maybe fifteen minutes, the other cats finally determined that I had been sequestered and thus represented no threat to their domain, so they went on about their business.

The big, black seniority cat—his name was Charlie—was lying down real stretched out on one of the steps about mid-way up the open stairwell that went out of their living room. I was a little curious about his positioning, but soon figured it all out.

One of the other cats approached the stairwell, went up a ways, and then came to a dead halt before reaching the big, black feline. Charlie didn't say anything, but with the look in his eyes and a quick flick of the tail, clearly and irrevocably indicated that this stairwell was *his* and that you didn't go up without *his* permission. It was like he had set up his own toll road and that the fee token was to first ask for passage, and then humble yourself before him so you might be granted the opportunity to pass by.

I got the idea that this first cat was in a big hurry and didn't observe proper procedures, as she suddenly did a flying leap kind of thing, avoiding the swatting paw of Charlie, and disappeared up in the second floor of the house.

Rather amazingly—and from my point of view, showing a total lack of respect on the part of the other cats—this happened *three more times* in the next hour! The last cat who did it brought Charlie to his feet after he had passed by. I knew this had been the last straw. He started down the steps with these deep, slow, elongated meows and headed toward his "owners" in the living room.

I felt sort of bad about the whole thing, but knew I didn't dare make even the slightest move, as reminding him of my presence in his territory—after what he had just gone through—would make matters much worse.

He finally made his way over to his "owners" and after a few leg swipes and an even louder meowing version of his distraught condition, they fortunately picked him up and gave him a little affection. "What's wrong, Charlie? Aren't you feeling well?"

It was like they thought he was sick to his stomach or something! Oh well, at least they picked him up. This sad-but-lucky turn of events interrupted the humans' conversation and got me out of the house and back to my own safe territory. As they did their farewell routines, lingering on like humans do, I heard the "lady owner" of the foreign house say, "*Animals* can be really strange at times, don't you think? *Our* Charlie suddenly gets ill for no reason at all, and *your* Fuzzy just lay there the whole time like a stuffed toy."

"Oh, right—that's just a *great* summary of what had transpired! I wonder how she came up with that amazing revelation! Strange *animals*, indeed."

Humans call us "animals" and I wouldn't mind the term so much if it weren't so often used in a disrespectful, condescending manner. For most of them, "animal" suggests something like "inferior, non-thinking, non-rational creature of low or no intelligence." So, how would *you* feel about that kind of label?

Humans even call each other "animals" on occasion when they

want to refer to another's uncouth or primitive kinds of actions. Just wonderful, huh! Makes all us cats look bad.

Let's analyze this bit by bit so we can maybe clear up this unjustified denigration once and for all. To begin with, how about the word "inferior." What does that mean? I think I've heard it comes out to something like "worse than." That's a negative, right?

So, the cat next door can't jump as high as I can. Or, the cat across the street has got a dark, mangy coat of fur that never seems to stay real clean and kempt. Therefore, they're "inferior." It's like jumping higher or lower or the exact kind of fur I have really had some kind of vital importance or significance in the realm of things. Does it?

I go on about how stupid mutts are all the time and call them an *inferior* species—and I'll probably keep on doing it because that's just a part of my character—but I'll tell you a little secret here before Snowball gets up to the porch and can hear me. Some of those dogs can be real sharp creatures! They can catch you completely off guard and send you rocketing up the nearest tree before you even knew what hit you—real heart attack time!

And then they'll keep you trapped high up there in those lonely, unsteady, swaying branches well after the point of desperation sets in—just for spite and amusement. I've never felt too "superior" when brought under those circumstances. But you didn't get that from me, okay?

We "animals" are "non-thinking and non-rational" too, according to popular belief. I've always wondered how humans arrived at that conclusion. I mean, *how do they know that we don't think?* Seriously now?

What if there were different kinds of thought processes, or

different "ways" to think? Would they know it if they saw it? And if they saw it, would they understand it? You can't understand what you don't know and worse yet, you can't know it if you aren't even looking for it. Is this getting too complex?

"Non-rational" is the thing that ticks me off the most. I've spent years trying to figure out exactly what "rational" means, at least in the human sense of the concept, and never have gotten anywhere with the subject.

For example, they often talk about "rational behavior." I once saw an old, decrepit dog stroll out onto a high-speed road just before a vehicle reached where he was crossing. He got hit and was immediately killed. Was that rational, or just non-thinking and stupid?

Wait—there's more to the story. For better or worse, I had the chance to look deep into that dog's eyes the moment before he took that final walk and from that, I knew that he had done it on purpose. He wanted to die. It was his choice. The eyes tell you everything if you know what to look for. That day they told me the sad tale of an aged, unloved, homeless, sick being who just didn't want to go on living anymore under those conditions. If cats could cry...

And what about the role of history—more specifically, of "time"—in this matter? Seeing Snowball here in my yard makes me think of human courtship. I understand that nowadays in many settings the gal can ask out the guy on a date, and even pay her own way. *Rational*, appropriate behavior, right? What about 50, or 100, or 200 years ago? Would that have been "rational" on the part of the girl? What would have been the reaction from the boy? From society? And 50, 100, or 200 years from now into the future, what will the "courtship code" be like?

Is it possible that there's some "time relativity" involved here, and with that in mind, is there *really* and *truly* such a thing as "rational," or does it more likely depend on the particular society, culture, education, upbringing, and time period involved? They say "beauty" is in the eyes of the beholder. Sort of like what suits our own personal tastes, needs, and comfort levels at the moment, don't you think?

One more thought. I see many humans routinely indulging themselves in all the physical comforts of life—bigger houses, faster transportation, more stylish clothes, the latest electronic gadgets—all the while communicating less, ignoring their emotional and intellectual enrichment, and caring only about themselves and their own personal whims and fancies. Is that "rational behavior"? Why is it so prevalent? Why doesn't anybody question it? Must be "rational" then, right?

Actually, I don't really care if they want to call this or the other thing "rational" or not. It's far beyond my understanding. What bugs me though is that with different circumstances, with different people, in different lands, at different times, they can do anything they want with this *rationality* concept to praise or demean others around them. Yet we cats, for all practical purposes and aspects, are simply and forever labeled as *non- rational beings.* We've never had it and never will. Figure that one out!

You know what? I forgot all about telling you about Snowball's visit to my house. You gotta remind me of these things or you'll miss out on the best part!

Okay, I'm concentrating now. Snowball made her way up to the steps and the first thing I've got to do is go through the proper cat greeting routine or she may think me stand-offish and unappreciative of her visit.

We did the classic "end-to-end, circle around, sniff-n-whiff, how-ya-been" cat thing. Although it may look rather strange and unappealing to humans, it's actually very thoroughly satisfying.

You see, it's a multi-faceted kind of greeting involving movement, sight, touch, and smell. It's pretty much exclusively practiced by the felines, and to some degree, by the canines—although with much less style. This might all be sort of tricky for humans to pull off without arousing a lot of suspicion on the part of any innocent bystanders. You'd better just stick to the handshake.

As I said, that was great! Snowball was looking, feeling, moving, and smelling as good as ever. Now that I've got that all checked out and confirmed, we can get down to business.

Hey, maybe she'll wanna scratch up the wooden planks on the porch with me! Yeah, we could make those neat little designs through the varnish just like the humans do with finger-painting. I'll start and see if she joins in. Yeah, that's it. Hey, there's a nice, smooth untouched part over on the other side too that "the owners" refinished last week. Let's do that area next!

That's why I like it went Snowball comes over—we're so tuned in to each other's likes and dislikes that it's just "cat compatibility heaven." Hey, where's she running off to? She's heading down the steps into the flower bed. Ah, I know. We're going to play "swat the petals off the roses" game. Okay, I'm coming. Wait for me! Yeah, pick out the biggest, most open ones. Swat! Got one. Look at that poor stem swing back and forth like a woozy punching bag. Swat! Got another one. It's trickier on the moving ones, but you gotta be up to a challenge to play this game. Swat! Swat! Swat! Swat

Whew! I guess we'll have to wait a few days until some more flowers come out before we can resume that little pastime activity. Hey, the "lady owner" is coming running out of the house. She must wanna greet Snowball since she hasn't been over for quite a while.

"Get *out* of my flower bed you awful cats! Just look what you've done—you've destroyed *every rose* on *every bush,* and I was going to cut them and bring them in the house tonight. What do you think..."

Her voice was already fading into the distance as it had suddenly occurred to me that this would be a good time to invite Snowball to go to the park down the street with me—making a quick exit.

Parks are fantastic places! There's so much for a cat to do there. This one we've got nearby my house is just chock full of these tall scratching posts that the humans call trees. Might as well start out with that activity since the floor planks on the porch are of a lower quality wood and tend to dull the ole nails a little.

"Hey Snowball, watch this!" I took a running leap at the tree in front of me and like a big suction cup on a glass plane, pegged myself to the bark about half-way up the trunk. I just hung there a little, then glanced over my back to see if she were taking it all in. Whoa, she began to run at my tree and then, yeah, she was coming flying up the trunk behind me.

Plop! I had simultaneously released all four claws and had done a perfect back flip to the ground, avoiding her ascending assault by a half second. I was off running like a turbo-powered snake, weaving and swerving among all the trees, with Snowball just a step behind me all the time and expertly following my every change of direction. Wow, she's really good!

I screeched to a halt in a mound of leaves, sending a bunch of them flying up into the air and, animated by the breeze, floating around above my head. Snowball had stopped beside me, eyeballs glued to all those airborne enemies that had been brought to life. "Okay," I said, "*let's get them!*"

We did some fantastically aerobatic leaps and spins, bringing the evil leaf gliders down once again to a sleeping submission among their dormant accomplices on the ground. We lay down a bit to rest now, as it had been a tiring though pleasurable victory.

"Hey, Snowball. I think I just saw a *flying saucer* over in the distance!"

"Ah, you're just tired and are imagining things. Why don't you take a little nap!"

"No, there it goes again, heading back the other direction now. I saw it *for sure* this time! Come on, let's go check it out."

We scurried through the trees heading for the open grassy area beyond, stopping at the edge of the woods so as to not be spotted by the alien crew should they want to beam us up or something.

"You see Snowball, there it goes back the other way. It's green and round and spinning and hey, some human grabbed ahold of it! Watch out! It'll use its laser beam and zap off your hand in one pass and..." Whew! He must have heard me because he threw it real hard and fast like. That was a close one because I've seen these movies on t.v. with the "owners" where this big spaceship...

"Fuzzy, *another human* just caught the thing! What kind of crazy people are there in this park today? I saw him—I think he caught it *on purpose*! Whoa, it must have zapped him or something because he let that thing fly off like nobody's business. That'll teach him to be more observant of what..."

"Snowball, the guy on *my side* grabbed the thing *again*! You're right—there are some real total lunatics in the park today. Come on. Let's get out of this area before it catches sight of us and zaps us too."

We went scampering back through the wooded area, rather uneasy about that last experience, and came out into another clearing that had a big pond in it.

"Hey Snowball, do you see that?"

"What are you talking about?"

"Over there. Look— there's a whole bunch of these huge, fat birds sitting by the side of the pond. They're just sitting there, looking sort of stupid like."

"Wow. Those *are* big birds! And they've got gigantic mouths on them, huh! How do you think they manage to sit up on tree branches like the ones around your house? That'd be a ridiculous looking sight, wouldn't it!"

We had a good laugh thinking about that image in our heads.

"I've got an idea, Snowball. I don't think they *can* sit up on tree branches. In fact, as big and fat as they are, I bet they can't even get off the ground without some booster rocket like the one I saw in that movie I was mentioning before about the spaceship. You see, to get a rocket off the ground, you... I'm getting distracted here. What we can do is head back into the trees, circle around to where they are, mount a super surprise attack, and *nab* one of those land blimps for a tasty little afternoon snack. What do you think?"

"Sounds like a great plan, Fuzzy. Let's go. You lead the way and I'll follow."

We did our best low-noise, crouched-down, sneak-up-on-the-enemy-fat-bird approach and soon were hiding behind the trees closest to where they were sitting. I knew this was going to be a piece of cake, as I could already taste the plump, succulent, juicy bird treat in my wildly salivating mouth. There was no reason to delay the feast—let the party begin!

"Okay, Snowball. Dig your claws into the ground real good. That's it. Now, crouch down low in front and get your back end high up in the air. I'm doing the same. Good. Next, tense up every muscle in your body as tight as you can possibly get it. Yes, I can feel it as I'm swaying back and forth from the pure energy force built up in my whole being! Now, ears back and fangs out! Okay, we're ready! On the count of three, give it everything you've got and go for the gold! One! Two! Threeeeeeeee!"

It was perfect. A blindingly fast, uniform start rocketed us out from behind the trees. Almost gliding over the ground at light speed, we observed that the targeted prey caught sight of us when we had reached about half of our desired striking distance, and began to quickly flutter their big, clumsy wings. We could see that even if they could somehow lift those enormous bodies off the ground, there was no way they could do it in time to fly away. Sweet victory would soon be upon us—and *in* us!

As we were just about to leap upon them, they elevated themselves ever so gently off their resting place and...

We screeched to a halt just before reaching the water, with looks of utter disbelief on our faces.

"Hey, Fuzzy. They jumped into the *water*—can you believe that! They'd rather *drown* themselves than go to battle or try to fly away! What kind of crazy bird is that anyway?"

Actually, I was thinking exactly the same thing, but before I could respond I began to notice that they weren't sinking. In fact, they seemed to be floating—and doing it rather well!

"What's going on, Snowball? And what's...that's the funniest sounding 'chirping' I've ever heard out of a bird! Hey, they're moving off, like they've got some water motor or something that propels them in the way they want to go. And now they're getting all lined up in what looks like some kind of advanced formation. Maybe we oughta just get out of here, huh."

With that, we decided to head back to my house where we could find normal, intelligent life again. It had been a strange afternoon, but I still had a happy feeling inside since I'd had the chance to spend it with Snowball. Whatever happened, we always had a good time together because we were two of a kind. Like two peas in pod. A true twosome.

This whole fat-bird-converting-into-a-motor-boat experience forced me to reflect on life a little and become a bit philosophical about things. I think it would do that to anyone, don't you?

My training and practice from the time I was a kitty had taught me many things, including how to precisely prepare myself for a forceful, expert attack on an unsuspecting meal. I had been educated by my mother cat in an *intelligent* way. I had become *intelligent* through her guidance.

Snowball and I had executed our assault with a precision that would have made any feline proud. It was a classic, "how-to" affair. There were no miscalculations in strategy. No misjudgments in tactics. No errors in implementation. We *intelligently* carried out every part down to the very last detail, yet in the end, were left with empty paws.

All of this makes me ask myself, "Just how smart is smart?" Or perhaps, "What is smart?" Or even better, "Am I asking the wrong question?"

I heard someone once say, "He's the most stupid intelligent person I've ever met!" I've never forgotten that exclamation because of its obvious logical inconsistency that makes you think there's something suspicious going on.

There was a story once of a human called Mr. Manager. He had been a super student in his day, completing all his studies in record time and always having the highest grades in his class. He went on to the university after graduating as top-of-his-class in high school. In his college courses, it was the same. He finished his bachelor's, master's, and doctorate in business management one after the other—always the best, always first. He was admired and/or envied by all the other students and his professors.

After finishing with school, he received hundreds of job offers from all the biggest, most prestigious companies—and having chosen the best of the best—he began to work as a top executive right from the start. He was the boss, the big cheese, the grand leader, a man among mice.

That first job lasted almost two years, and then he was fired. Actually, I think he was given the opportunity to "resign," but the result was the same. He immediately received another high-level management position in another company, still basking in the benefits of his past educational performance. This second one lasted just a little more than one year, and he was let go again.

The third position was of a little lower level now, and he only made it for six months this time. Finally, by the fifth job assignment he was no longer in charge of anyone and had been forced to accept a rather menial post with a rather average company. This was now the only kind of thing he good get, just to keep a minimal paycheck coming in to be able to meet the monthly bills. It seems he had done everything exactly right too, but in the end, never caught the fat bird.

The only thing I can figure out is this: some humans, like Mr. Manager, get all this *formal, theoretical* super-detailed, advanced training through their schools and then go out into the world hunting jobs and never really catch one.

On the other hand, some felines get all this *informal, practical* super-detailed, advanced training through their mother cats and then go out in the world hunting birds and never really catch one either.

It's gotta be a problem of "extremes"—what else could it be? You go too far one way or the other, and you either can't see the forest for the trees, or the trees for the forest.

It seems that there are *both* trees and forest, although in the end they are either collectively or individually *exactly the same thing*. That's a strange kind of logic, isn't it! I guess that's *Fuzzy Logic*.

How smart is smart? Just a happy medium, thank you.

Working for a living

Chapter Five

The Great Horde of Avenging Chihuahuas resumed its march through the once-tranquil cat territories, heading directly toward the Feline Kingdom. They reached the outer limits in a week and a half, faster than had been predicted, finding only abandoned outposts with no signs of feline resistance to their entry. This encouraged them even more and filled their beast brains with a violent, savage confidence never seen in those parts before.

Chucky the Chihuahua, the huge, gruesome leader, led them on at a frightening pace that would have tired and debilitated most dog armies of that time. In this case, however, they seemed to gain more strength with each step since they were all so fully energized with the thoughts of a swift, easy victory and a plentiful bounty to come at the end of their trail. It was a powerful, horrible sight to behold.

As the thousands of wiry, pointy-helmeted canines marched along, they threw up a cloud of dust and created a reverberating paw-to-Earth pounding that could be seen and heard far off into the distance. It was like "doom" had taken a physical form and been projected directly into all those sinewy little bodies.

They moved in perfect unison, kept in sync by the repetitive singing in their high, ear-piercing, squeaky little voices of their specially written war ballad.

"Strong, valiant Chihuahuas march,
soon, to make, the cats' backs arch.
With a heave, a ho, a snarl, a bite,
the Feline Kingdom'll be ours tonight!"

And so on they sang, becoming more self-confident and assured with each hideous repetition. The furry was boiling in the blood of their little pulsating veins, and their eyes popped out wide with a dreadful look of savage determination. They knew they were ready, and ready they were.

All were focused in on that mythical and hated figure of Fuzzy the Great, as they knew that if he were to fall victim of their deadly fangs, their sharp swords, or their pointy helmets, that everything and everybody else would fall with him in one swift blow. Fuzzy the Great was the key. Fuzzy the Great was the target. Fuzzy the Great must be eliminated!

"Strong, valiant Chihuahuas march,
soon, to make, the cats' backs arch.
With a heave, a ho, a snarl, a bite,
the Feline Kingdom'll be ours tonight!"

The Avenging Horde of Chihuahuas hoped to reach the gates of their destination in less than two-weeks time. A very *short* two weeks for those felines who were about to face the biggest challenge of their long and glorious history. A very short two weeks indeed!

Meanwhile, back in the Feline Kingdom, preparations for the soon-to-be-assault were being carried out at a frantic pace. All of the cats were having each and every one of their claws sharpened to a fine, strong point. Rigorous exercise sessions were rotated among the population and repeated every two hours to refine abilities in jumping, spinning around, climbing, back arching, crouching, hissing, and swatting. This not only was bringing them up to top *physical* condition, but also permitted them to hone their skills in *mental* concentration and awareness. It was truly "all for one and one for all."

Fuzzy the Great was busy on his own, having climbed to the top of one of the towers of his castle to be able to silently meditate on the formulation and carrying out of his plan. This plan would have to be like no other plan ever conceived of before because he knew, as did all around him, that they were vastly outnumbered in this epic struggle for survival.

This fact of life was of course left unspoken during the preparations. When they talked, and there was very little of that, they spoke of their proud, long history and how any and all challenges in the past had always been somehow met victoriously and thus must once again reach the same glorious conclusion.

The sporadic conversations were indeed optimistic and of the most positive nature, but deep inside their eyes you could see the very anguishing concern that touched every part of their being. They knew, as did their valiant leader, that this would be the test of their lives. This would be the battle for their lives.

Fuzzy the Great mused on the concept of the Chidozer that he had proposed during his speech just a short time ago. This seemed to be the only way, the only possible way to have a chance of turning back and, if all went well, defeating once and for all the Avenging Horde of Chihuahuas. He knew that this plan would have to be formulated with a detail and precision that left no room for error, or they would simply be overrun by this excessively numerous band of snarling beasts.

After one more full day of intense thought and preparation, Fuzzy the Great had all the pieces in place in his mind and called together a team of the best artisans from amongst the cat citizenry. They solemnly met around an enormous, oval wooden table that was located in the center of his stone-walled dining area. A fire was burning brightly in the fireplace at one end, which served to illuminate the room and send a feeling of warmth through their tired, aching bodies in these last rather cool days of spring.

The room was filled with a nervous, silent anticipation as each guest was appropriately greeted and escorted to his chair. When all had finally arrived and been seated, Fuzzy the Great took his place at the head of the table, and remaining standing, began to speak.

"My friends, I have called you here today for reasons in general that you are well aware of and I will not waste your time by reiterating the urgency of the task that lies before us. Specifically, you as a group have been selected because of your advanced skills in construction and mechanics. You are the artisans of our Kingdom and this moment requires of you to bring forth of yourselves, to rise to the utmost height of your abilities. Our very survival depends on it!"

"Your task, under my direction and guidance, is to build a most important and sophisticated device called the Chidozer. There is no previous model to draw ideas from because this is a new and untested concept that has sprung forth from my head in an effort to find a way to defend ourselves against these thousands of Chihuahua beasts that will soon be upon us."

"There is no previous example of its effectiveness since this will be the first of its kind. Therefore, we must construct this under the faith and hope that with no test-runs, no simulations, no mock battles, it will serve the purpose it has so duly been designed to carry out."

"If I am expressing myself clearly, you will understand that this is a one-time, unproved conceptual opportunity to find our way to victory."

"I have faith in you because I have faith in the species, 'cat.' I know that you will work hard and relentlessly to complete this project according to specifications and on time because this has now been defined as your *duty*, and a cat always accomplishes his task in fine form."

"The construction will take place in the wide, open field that lies behind my castle walls, and when finished, the Chidozer will be transported to a secret holding place in the center of our Feline Kingdom. There it will wait to be put into action at the appropriate moment."

Fuzzy the Great went on in great detail for approximately three hours. He explained the strategies involved for its use against the Chihuahuas. He gave details on the tactics that would be implemented in its operation. He formed a team from the group that had arrived that would be in charge of its workings during the battle itself and later started them in training exercises so they could smooth and perfect their skills.

He brought together other teams that would be responsible for specific parts of the Chidozer's construction, carefully assigning each member according to his abilities. Detailed sketches were shown and meticulously outlined for them, so as to assure that it would function well and correctly from the start, since there would be no time for second efforts or attempts.

When all had been made clear and everyone knew exactly what he was to do, the work began. The project took shape quickly over the next few days as they labored tirelessly into the wee hours each morning, carrying on under the bright lights of bonfires scattered about the open field.

Fuzzy the Great moved among his crew at every moment with a vigor and air of confidence that filled them all with the energy and hope necessary to toil well beyond their normal physical abilities. Things were progressing well, but time was short, and the enemy was strong.

We would soon see if this plan would result in their salvation and be transformed into another grand episode in the Feline Kingdom's long, illustrious history, or if it would represent the final unwritten chapter of a once-great land that had perished under its valiant but fruitless efforts for survival.

This would be a fight to the death, with nothing in between winning or losing. There would be no peace treaties, no negotiated settlements, no accords reached. There would be no prisoners taken, no dwellings spared, no corner left untouched. There would be no, "we shall rise again to fight another day," or regroupings, rearmament, or lulls in the battle.

In the end, there would only remain a victor, because the loser would simply cease to exist. The last hope would vanish with the last breath, and those left standing would remain with the spoils. It was really "all or nothing" and not "all for one and one for all."

That was the code of war—at least, the code of the Chihuahuas' kind of war. The objective was not defeat, for that left the defeated with the ever-present possibility of someday rising up once again in arrogant defiance. They knew that history was long and time was kind to those with patience and perseverance. "What comes around, goes around," as they say.

In fact, time was normally on the side of the defeated, for history tells us that the victors often become careless and soft over the years, looking with blind eyes at the growing strength of their previously subdued and oppressed enemy. As the formerly victorious wallow in the pleasures of their spoils, a dark cloud of vengeance slowly builds up and takes shape among those who had been humiliated until one day, springing forth from careful planning and the imminent power of a deep-ingrained and ever-lasting hatred, it explodes into an uncontrolled violence that the once-strong and valiant conquerors are not prepared to defend themselves against.

With that, the two opposing groups often change their respective roles of winner and loser, rewriting history in a most abrupt and absurd kind of way. And if the "new" loser should only be subdued into defeat—to survive and live amongst *his* victors—it is very probable that at some time in the future the whole process will rear up its ugly head and repeat itself once again!

So is the understanding of war of the Chihuahuas. And so is the justification of their brutal objectives. Agreeable or not, likable or not, ethical and humane or not, it was definitively and clearly logical in its discourse.

This guiding philosophy was precisely the manner in which they had achieved such great stature and power, and why they were so feared by all who knew of their feats. A proposed attack by the Avenging Horde on any group immediately brought about pounding pains of fear in the hearts of their targeted victims.

Interestingly enough, the Chihuahuas' warring abilities and tactics were so strongly ingrained in their very being that only the threat of an attack often brought their enemies to their knees, at least figuratively speaking, even before the first blow had been struck.

With that to their advantage, the rest was relatively easy, and this is what brought about their many rather unexpected lightening-fast victories in times of battle. It was psychological warfare with the very real support of a physical pounding. And it was all done in a professional and deadly-serious way.

It can now be seen how devastating a force the cats were truly facing. There was no turning back because destiny had already marked the place and the moment. "Destiny," in this case, went by the name of "Chihuahua." The place was the Feline Kingdom, and the moment would be soon, very soon.

What was to be, would be. And so it was written.

Whoa! Where am I? What's going on? What am I doing here? I need to get to the castle immediately because the Chihuahuas...! Castle? Chihuahuas? What castle? And who cares about some slinky, wining little... Wow, I must have been...

I think I chowed down too much of that cut-up fish this morning before my morning nap. I need to be more careful about that. Maybe I should just sit here a little while and try to collect my thoughts because I'm feeling a little disoriented at the moment.

Okay, I think I'm getting my senses back. That was a close one! Well, I can see that the "owners" have taken off for the day and left me here as usual to take care of everything. I know it's *my* house and everything, but if they're going to share the place with me, they could at least be a little more responsible and watch over the dwelling a little more often. But no, they've got "other things to do"! "Responsibilities" I think they're called. I'm sure glad I'm not in their shoes.

Work, work, work, work. That's all they do. They say it brings *meaning* to their lives, fulfillment, emotional rewards, but personally, I have my doubts. I think it's really just about occupying their time, and, about *money*.

And money isn't even really the *end*, but rather the *means* to other things. It's the link, the bridge, the way to. Alone, money is rather useless. It's just paper or metal stuff that gets your paws dirty if you touch it too much. But as a "medium of exchange," as they say, now that's where things get interesting! *Really* interesting! In fact, that's what it's all about—*exchange*.

Like when I catch a nice, juicy, crackling, crunchy lizard outdoors in the backyard. What do I do—do I kill it off right away and put it out of its miserable reptile existence? No, of course not! I just slap it around enough to make it dizzy and slower, and then bring it right in the house into the living room!

It's all about *exchange*, don't you see? The "owners" have been giving me that cut-up fish in little round cans every day, so I thought I'd offer them something in return for all their kindness. I stroll happily into the house, hold up the "catch of the day" right in plain sight in front of them, and meow, "Hey, take a gander at this, guys. I brought you a present!"

I've learned, unfortunately though, that the idea of *exchange* seems to depend a lot on something called "mutual satisfaction." You see, somehow in the scheme of things, "fish" for "lizard" just doesn't come out as an equitable deal—at least in the eyes of my "owners."

I always figured they were getting the best part of the bargain 'cause the food I *brought in* was *alive* and still "huntable"—thus much more attractive and inviting for the palate. On the other hand, the fish they regularly broke out was tasty—don't get me wrong—but it was always sleeping and provided for no sharpening of the warrior skills built into us. Sort of boring and unchallenging, if you know what I mean.

Well, the reaction was always the same. The "lady owner" would do this kind of shrieking, jumping thing off the couch when she saw my lizard, inevitably wildly flinging across the room anything that might have happened to be in her hands at the moment.

The "man owner," whose first natural reaction would seemingly be exactly the same, quickly brings himself under control and with an uneasy smile will say something like, "Oh, look what Fuzzy's caught!" The lady screams back, "I can see what Fuzzy's caught, and I want you to get it out of here right now!"

I've learned that when reptiles or insects are involved and both the male and female of the human species are present, it's the male type who is always assigned the task of capture and removal. Probably some kind of "code" or "rule" that they gotta follow.

The "man owner" usually does okay taking care of the various crickets, spiders, and other assorted vermin I bring in for show and exchange, as he's pretty quick about it and maintains this look of self-confidence on his face.

I get the feeling though that he's not a big lizard fan because with these, he's always first saying stuff like, "Now be a good Fuzzy and just take that back out to where you found it." That's my cue to drop it on the carpet, of course, and get a little short-lasting pleasure of seeing it begin to squirm around as it slowly gets its senses back.

No, this whole "exchange" thing is tough for us cats. Like, what else can we do for *trade* if even a juicy, live lizard doesn't get them to participate? This stupid mutt next door has his own "system" with this rubbery, bouncy ball.

He brings the thing up to his "owner," handing it to him all slobber-covered and disgusting, then jumps around in circles barking like he's gone completely insane, until the "owner" heaves it off into the distance. With that, he runs like the furry, as if not catching this spherical irritant would be the end of the world, and brings it right back to where he started again. Can you believe that?

And on and on it goes, until either the "owner" runs out of ambition or the poor mutt runs out of breath. Fun "exchange," right!

Imagine a *cat* doing something like that! It just wouldn't look cool, don't you know. We've got some dignity to hold up here, and can't be zooming around like crazy beings with tongues hanging out and dribbling all over everything and everybody. We're lightening fast and can catch-and-fetch with the best of them, but it's gotta be done with "style" and "elegance," or just not done at all!

The "owners" got me a little rubber ball one day—one of those super-bouncy ones that seems to have a mind of its own about which direction it's going to go next. Devilish little things, I must say.

I screamed out, "Don't do it!", but the "owner" gives it a throw in the kitchen anyway and the thing goes nuts, bouncing from here to there, side to side, up and down. I just hung tight for a few seconds, trying my best to avoid giving myself whiplash by following it around with my head, and then I sprung into action with the utmost skill. Even with that, it took me a good minute to track the fiend down and lock it firmly between my jaws.

Don't they know that cats want controlled, tranquil environments? Anything that moves, especially in that kind of way, just breaks down all equilibrium and simply must be captured and subdued so as to return the place to normal.

Seeing that I had completed my mission, the "owner" says, "Okay, good Fuzzy. Now give it back to me and we'll do it again."

"Again!" I meowed, "Are you *crazy* or something? It was no easy feat to grab this thing the first time and be darned if we're going to willingly let it loose in my territory a second time!"

I quickly strutted out of the kitchen, the ball securely clamped in my mouth, and went right under the couch where I knew the thing could be permanently stored, safe from human intervention and reactivation. (They move the couch maybe once a year, so...) I heard the "owner" mutter something about "arrogant, non-sociable cat," but ignored his total lack of understanding as usual.

Humans get off on things like that sometimes. Repetitive tasks, mundane actions, mindless activities—I've seen it over and over again. Makes me think I'm watching an old movie because it's just a continual playback of stuff I've seen before. Why is that?

They say, "I need a challenge in life." Or, "My job offers me no challenge; it's just too boring." But when a *real* challenge presents itself, they're moaning and groaning about how difficult it is, how long it will take, how much it will cost, how they don't deserve this, how it's unfair that they should have to face this alone, how...just a whole bunch of griping "hows"—which means that they're upset that their comfortable routine has been so cruelly and unexpectedly shattered.

So which is it—do they want a "challenge" or not? Or is it just a "little, safe, not-too-tough challenge that they could resolve in five minutes but will spend three weeks with so they can look important, blow off some time, and feel-good-about-themselves kind of thing"? Non-threatening and a no-brainer—how about that?

It's like the other day there was a big conversation between my "man owner" and "lady owner." The man begins by saying, "I have to talk to you about my job. I can't take it anymore. It's just the same ole thing day after day, week after week, month after month, ..." The lady interrupts while squirming a little in her chair and not wanting to go through "year after year," "decade after decade," "century after century," and so on, and replies, "So, look for another job."

Wow, I was impressed—a short, sharp, quick answer that went right to the heart of the problem! I was about to walk off, thinking the whole issue had been resolved, when the man comes back with, "Another job! Are you serious? I've been with this company for ten years now, and I've got a pension plan. I've worked my way up in the organization, and you know, at my age, it isn't so easy to just go out and start over again."

"So, ask to be transferred to another department."

Kazamm—she did it again! This "lady owner" of mine has obviously got her thinking cap on today!

I was on my way out a second time, when, believe it or not, I noticed that the "man owner" had become even more perplexed—screwing up his face in strange, serious contortions.

"Ask for a transfer! Do you think that's so easy? And to what department? It's not like I'm a Jack-of-all-trades, you know! And even if I could, I'd surely have to start at the bottom again, maybe even taking a salary cut, and then working under some wet-behind-the-neck, know-it-all new recruit who thinks he is God's gift to mankind! How do you think I'd feel? Another department! I can't believe that..."

Squirming a little again, she replied, "So if you don't want to change *companies* and you don't want to change *within* the company you're at, what's left?"

Yep, excellent summary and counter-point—went right to the heart again! I might as well stick around awhile, 'cause the "lady owner's" really got her analytic act together today. Just good left-brain action, shooting to kill from the hip.

"That's exactly the problem!", retorted the man, as if he had come upon this grand revelation all by himself. "There's no way out. It's a one-way street. It's a dreary, dark dead end. It's..."

As you can imagine, super squirming was occurring on the lady's part, so she felt the obligation to interject something, anything, just to get off that road to nowhere, that tunnel with no end, that bottomless pit—sorry, I just couldn't resist!

"So, how can I help you? What do you want me to say? You tell me you're bored and need a challenge...,"—Ooh, did you hear that "challenge" word pop up again?—"but, then you shoot down every idea I give you. I don't know *what* you want!"

Okay, that was pretty good. Sort of said out of frustration and no big message was communicated there, but she did raise the appropriate questions and put the ball clearly in his court.

"I don't know. I just know that I need a *change*, but I can't see anyway to bring it about. Well, don't worry about it, honey, it's probably just 'one of those days' and I'll feel better about things tomorrow. You wanna go for an ice cream or something?"

No, no, no—what a wimpy comeback and conclusion! He'll "feel better tomorrow," he says. Maybe so, but *that's not the point*! The deal is, he's afraid of the "challenge," which means, he afraid of "change." How about that—that's an analysis that would make the "lady owner" proud!

Let me spell it out for you, since I lost my supporting cast with the ice cream turn of events—and mind you, I'm talking about *humans* here since us *cats* don't have to deal with this banal stuff.

You see, the humans—they gotta work. "Work" is a given. It all ties in to this "money" thing which ties in to this "exchange" thing. That oughta be self-evident, right?

The problem is, repetitive tasks lead to skills but also to boredom, so a *challenge* is sought out. But *challenge* means *change* and humans fear change because *change* means *risk*. Am I going too fast?

Unless of course it's just a "little" change, but in that case there's no real challenge, and we quickly get back to the boredom thing again. Sounds like the "viscous circle" expression the humans use although I never quite understood the meaning. The word "viscous" for me stirs up some faint but powerful image of Chihuahua dogs, but maybe I'm just imagining this or something.

Anyway, are you following me here? I'm trying to make this as simple as possible, to avoid doing a "man owner" kind of going nowhere conversation.

Boiling this all down to the bare essentials, the *real* problem is "fear," which is a derivative of "risk." If there were no risk or no fear of risk, there would simply be no problem, don't you see!

Under this point of view, "challenges" vis-a-vis "changes" would be okay kinds of things because the risk or fear thereof would just not be a relevant factor that stopped them dead in their tracks every time.

Since "risk" is real and in itself cannot be eliminated in the *physical* environment, then the obvious and only resolution of the problem lies in the elimination or at least reduction of the "fear" associated with the risk in the *emotional* environment. Yeah, I'm probably speeding down the highway on this one, but try to stay with me here.

Thus, we've got "givens" of work, money, exchange, repetition, skills, boredom, challenges, change, and fear. They're all real—in one way or another—but the *last* one is the key. It's the one that makes or breaks the "circle." It's the one the humans have got to deal with—direct and up front.

"Fear" is the enemy. It's what messes up the otherwise fairly agreeable and satisfying chain of events. With a swift sword, strong shield, and a Chidozer, one could...wow, I don't where these images are coming from, but I'd better leave it at that or you'll think I'm going crazy.

Whew! Short, sharp, and quick. The "lady owner" would surely give me a good pat on the back for that. Sorry she wasn't around to hear all this.

It could be said that us cats work too, but perhaps not in the way as would be known in the most common *human* understanding of the term. You see, I think for the majority of humans, work gets tied in too much to all that money-chain thing that we were talking about before.

For a cat, work could be thought of as the opposite of rest, which really just means, "activity." I'm trying to come up with some kind of equivalent concept here even though one doesn't exist.

Humans have activities too, but they like to separate and classify them into categories like work, eating, sports, games, reading, and so on. And then they further separate these categories in sub-categories and those sub-categories into others.

They're all just "things to do" as you can see, but the classification allows them to attach emotions and importance to each one. They're like hierarchies grouped by a range of feelings. If you want to know the truth, that's where they get into trouble so often and why they construct and ride their own private roller coasters, like I mentioned before. The roller coasters aren't real, but they sure take them for a ride at times!

We cats, as sensitive creatures and leaving the emotions behind, do what we need to do and don't worry about it, or evaluate its significance, or think about how we *feel* when we are doing it. If it's gotta be done, well then, it's gotta be done! What else is there to take into consideration, really?

It's like when you see a nice, new silk blouse temptingly hanging in the closet, with the door wide open. I can hear it calling to me, inviting me to come in. Every instinct in my body tells me that I must change from a state of "rest" to one of "activity" and immediately go over and check it out.

I'll make an easy and short leap to grab ahold of it with my claws, yanking if off the hanger and bringing it down to verification level on the floor below. Wow, it's smooth and soft! I may do a little dance on top of it, and then knead it up real good with my front claws so it gets all fluffy and bunched up. With that I can lie down on top of it for a long nap if left undisturbed, enjoying its luxurious, comforting fabric. No *emotions* involved here—I'm just taking caring of business!

Another required and non-hierarchical activity that comes up, is subduing leaves to a state of submission. The "owners" seem to get the "indoors" all confused with the "outdoors" and want to put these potted plant things in some of the rooms of my house. What's that all about anyway?

They say it gives the place "a rugged, natural ambiance" and "respirates the house." Well, if you want a really captivating "atmosphere," then just hang up some pictures of *me* on the walls! And if you really need to "let the structure breathe," I think opening up a few windows might just do the trick, don't you think!

That's humans for you—make the simple complicated and just go out and spend a bunch of money so they can complain more about having to work just to make ends meet.

It all started a few months ago when they visited a "nursery." I heard them say it, "Let's go to the *nursery* today." I immediately assumed I had missed out on the big event and they were going to come back with a screaming, burping little baby, but lo and behold, they filled the vehicle with *plants*! I think they sort of got mixed up on that one, but I didn't say anything to them.

Well, these outdoor things were distributed around the indoors, with much discussion involved regarding the "ideal location"—taking into account the possible projection of the sun's rays, shadow areas, viewing points, window positions, walking paths, Feng Shui, and who knows what else.

It appears there is advanced knowledge and study related to this interior transformation that is well beyond the natural abilities of the average feline. I let them go about their business, knowing that I'd probably have just grouped them all together to create a nice, little forest that one could creep into and hide in. They didn't see it from the practical point of view.

Once everything had been properly arranged in its place, the "owners" slumped down on the couch, exhausted from all their trials and tribulations. Now it was my turn!

First, let's check out the dirt! I hopped up into one of the bigger pots and felt the soil beneath my pads. Yep, this was the *outdoor* stuff alright! They looked upon this with suspicious eyes, but didn't say anything until I suddenly began to dig a nice, big whole in the pot with my front paws, thinking that if this worked out, this might save me a trip upstairs from time to time where they left this box with sand in it for me.

The most logical actions in the world, I've come to learn, are often unappreciated and misunderstood by humans. They threw a fit! They chased me out of the pot—and the room, for that matter—yelling something about, "Don't you know where the bathroom is!"

Well *of course* I know where the *bathroom* is—it's where you find the closest digable spot when the urge calls! And that's why I was checking this out *now* so as to not have to make a snap decision *later on* when the urge really was calling at full volume! Wasn't that obvious? Couldn't they see my advanced planning and careful preparation?

And then there are the *leaves*! I had naturally assumed that they formed a permanent part of the plant—one for all and all for one—but soon found out that from time to time, and without warning, would liberate themselves from their brethren and go crashing to the floor with a most devious swerving and floating movement.

That is always most disconcerting, as you don't really know if the foul and renegade leaf plans to take off on its own and scurry about the room, or if it will just lie there in a motionless silence.

The required response is of course to go and investigate. I don't go up too fast anymore because once in a while the leaf is encouraged and motivated by an invading breeze that whisks through a nearby window—bringing it up suddenly to flutter about—which can scare the heebie jeebies out of an innocent, unsuspecting feline.

At other times, it remains calm so that I can carefully and cautiously give it a few swats with my able right paw, verifying that this one, at least for the moment, seems to pose no immediate danger for the inhabitants of my dwelling.

There are sure *a lot* of leaves on those plants that they mistakenly brought back from the nursery! A lot of leaves means Fuzzy has to be on the alert and ready to go into action at a moment's notice, anytime of the day. And you humans think you've got it tough! Oh well, it's all in a day's work.

Let the good times roll

Chapter Six

"That was fun!", they said. If you want to know the truth, I was left totally frustrated by the whole evening's events. We had it *all*, *everything*, and then just gave it away as if it had no significance or importance! I don't know what happened, but we went from being lord of the city to a poor pauper in the street.

You see, it all started when those "neighbor owners" came over last night. *They* got this whole thing going. Everything was calm and quiet around my house before *they* showed up.

My "man owner" was watching one of his usual "sweaty events" on t.v. and the "lady owner" was deeply involved in one of those psychotic, unending conversations with herself while sitting all alone with this curved plastic thing against her ear. Yours truly was just lounging around on the carpet, keeping an occasional eye out for any renegade leaves or invading insects. Everything cool, right!

Suddenly there was a knock on the door. In they came with this *box* tucked under their arms. That made me suspicious from the get-go, but I didn't say anything at the moment. You know how "boxes" are. A long-standing house rule in any part of the world is that anytime a new box comes into one's dwelling, it must be immediately and thoroughly sniffed out and if possible—entered into—so as to verify its contents and intentions. One can even sleep it in a while if the "feeling" is right and no danger has been identified.

I stood up, alert, ready to carry out the procedure with total seriousness and dedication, but they just ignored me. All previously described activities were interrupted and the "box" was plopped down on my dining room table, where they all took their places.

This made me think this cardboard invader may actually not have bad intentions, but instead be the sacred transporter of some kind of food item that might be of interest to both humans and cats alike. Better keep a close eye on things!

Well, they wasted a good ten minutes with what I believe they call, "casual conversation." I was meowing all the time, "Hey, open it up! You got some food in there, or what?" Finally, they took off its hat and exposed the contents. I jumped up on an extra chair at the table so I could get a full view of what was going on.

"Oh, look!", exclaimed the "neighbor lady owner." "How cute! Your Fuzzy wants to play with us!"

"*Play* with you—in your *dreams*! Just pull up a plate to where I'm sitting and I'll go about my business and be outta here in no time!"

Much to my surprise and chagrin, this was *not* a food box. Not a morsel, a piece, a crumb—nothing! But, it had a bunch of curious-looking stuff inside, so I decided to stick around for a little bit to see if there was anything swattable or attackable—to at least salvage this whole falsely built-up expectation in some way or another.

First, the "neighbor man owner" pulled out this heavy cardboard thing, unfolded it to form a nice square, and placed it in the middle of the table. It seemed everyone but me knew what was going on because while I watched with increasing interest, they were just jabbering on incessantly about all kinds of unimportant topics that had absolutely nothing to do with the unveiling of the box's contents. Sort of sacrilegious, don't you think?

After that, these funny-looking, poorly designed, small bills of money were distributed equally among all present. I tried to warn my "lady owner" next to me, meowing under my breath, "Hey, these neighbors of ours are *counterfeiters*! Yeah, I saw this same thing on a detective show once. Run! Get out of here *now* before it's too late!"

She either didn't hear me or just wanted to "live on the wild side that night" because she went right on jabbering away as if nothing suspicious at all were taking place.

Next, each person got his own "piece" that seemed to be sort of a big deal to select. Something about some pieces being more "lucky" than others, or that, "I always play with *that* piece." Who cares about the "piece"! I want to know more about this fake money stuff and how they think they're gonna pass off those ugly replications to anybody except maybe a blind person or a space alien. Maybe the neighbors got zapped in the head by that flying saucer Snowball and I saw in the park the other day and have since lost all sense of reality! I'd better keep watching.

Following the ceremony of the distribution of the "pieces," the "neighbor man owner" dumped out a whole bunch of plastic, miniature houses and hotels on the table and piled them up in a very unorganized, topsy-turvy little neighborhood beside him. What did they have to do with anything? I've seen little kid humans regularly playing with things like that, but at least they know how to put all the structures right-side-up and make decent-looking rows with streets and stuff like that. This guy had obviously had a deprived childhood and had no idea of what he was doing or how silly his display looked.

Last, two tiny, square white blocks with dots on them were brought out and handed to my "lady owner," saying that she could "go first." I was starting to get up, thinking we'd "go" together and thus take advantage of the opportunity to dissociate ourselves from the badly counterfeited money, but instead, she just sat there calmly and then threw the little cubes onto the table in front of her.

"Don't worry, I'll get them!" I shouted. I pounced up on the table and with a quick swat of my right paw, sent one of the shiny, slick little devils rocketing off the table and into the living room. Honing in on its twin brother and about to do the same to the second one, my "lady owner" screamed out, "No, Fuzzy! Leave them alone! Get down off that table now and behave yourself!"

I was physically—and rudely—escorted back to my chair while my "man owner" went to retrieve the enemy cube I had so adeptly sent running for its life. "Just go again," she was told, and this time I didn't even bother to get up since I was beginning to get the idea that my "owners" were somehow mysteriously implicated in this counterfeiting operation.

The white blocks were sent tumbling across the table once again and some "number" was strangely announced when they had come to a halt. My "lady owner" subsequently moved her private "piece" on the square board in the middle of the table, and then the white blocks were passed to the "neighbor lady owner." Surprisingly, she followed the same procedure, although they announced a different "number" for her.

This rather disconcerting and curious rite was repeated again and again, like all had been put under some kind of trance and were unconsciously submitting to its evil spell.

I was about to get out of there—thinking those satanic cubes may lay an eye on me next—when things suddenly got *real* interesting. It seems that at certain undetermined times—for what I could figure out—one could take that worthless, poorly reproduced money that had been handed out and buy houses and hotels! That's what they said at least—"I'll buy a hotel!"

And those little toy structures must be like "deeds" for the later transferal of the real buildings to their proper buyers. I never saw anything like that with the kid humans. These adult games must be more sophisticated even though they use the same kinds of toys sometimes.

You know what? Maybe my owners know what they're doing after all! We could end up with a summer home, a winter home, a vacation home, and some hotels for when you just feel like getting away from it all! Yeah, I could get into that!

Okay, concentrate now. See if you can get us some more of those little plastic buildings. We'll just get the neighbors to print up some more of that money if you run out or something. This is easier than I thought!

Well, the board-based real estate ceremony went on and on into the evening, taking ever stranger turns of events. Sometimes one human would get to buy more buildings, and other times he would have to just hand them over to one of the other humans—and without proper compensation, I tell you!

For a while, my "lady owner" was like "Queen of the Table," as she had accumulated this huge group of structures all over the place. I was already making plans as to which new house I would invite Snowball to first, and envisioning a possible list of locations for construction in general so we could optimize our pleasure.

As the evening went on though, the mean, greedy "neighbor man owner" began to take control and by the time all was said and done, he had cruelly and sadistically captured every little house and hotel on that board. It was an *awful* sight!

I jumped down from my chair, totally frustrated as I had mentioned earlier, and just slinked over to my nearest cat bed to lie down and wallow in my misery.

What had happened? I had stuck around and given them the proper cheerleading and full moral support. They could've quit when they had a whole bunch of those houses and hotels, but no, they just kept playing and playing and playing until they lost them all!

What is it about humans anyway? Why are they like that? What is this "all or nothing" thing that I hear about and see so often? Is there no *middle* road? Can't *everybody* win and *nobody* lose sometimes? Is that so complicated or difficult?

How about in sports? Well, they aren't exactly set up for the win-win kind of battle, at least not *directly*. In golf, for example, the one who gets that aggravating little moon-surfaced alien egg to go into the hole in the fewest whacks is the winner. Only one *really cool* trophy and *big* check handed out per tournament, right!

In basketball, it's the fivesome who plunges the big orange through the lacy donut the most times that enjoys the victory. If you didn't win, then you must have...

Football revolves around running and bumping up and down a green area with a much sought after oval tribute to a dead pig. Sort of prehistorically ritualistic—as far as the strategic serenading of the ball goes—but there is still only *one* triumphant group of giants when the last whistle blows.

Can't they *both* win—the loser getting something out of it at least *indirectly*? Maybe "losses" could build character, or teach one to learn from one's mistakes, or motivate one to improve oneself, or just not be "felt" as a loss at all. How about if one just played the game for the sheer *pleasure* of it, or for the *exercise*, or the satisfying *challenge* that was associated with it in general?

From what I've seen, some humans *try* to think that way—and if you ask them, they look you straight in the eyes and say that this is *exactly* how they view and play sports. They say it, but you know what? However much they try to convince themselves that winning or losing doesn't matter, there's always that little extra gleam in their eyes when they've come out on the victor's end!

And if by some chance—due either to luck or natural talents and abilities—they happen to really put their opponent away in dramatic and stinging fashion, the overflowing exhuberation springing forth from within is almost impossible to disguise or hold back. Sort of embarrassing for the guy who's been trying to sell everyone on his true "love of sports for sports sake."

No, the hypocrisy always leaks out into the open when the humans try to deny that which they instinctively are. It's in the genes, don't you see? Many things are like that—a lot of qualities, reactions, and feelings that most humans would rather have shed through hereditary deselection and kicked out of the gene pool. Sorry to inform you, but that's sort of out of your control—for the moment, at least.

Maybe that's why we lost all the hotels and houses we had acquired in that confusing table game I was watching. My "lady owner" could've been thinking, "Just a *couple* more houses and hotels, and then I'll take my winnings and go home." And "a couple" never quite gets clearly defined or reached.

Or, "Just *one more round*." And round and round and round...

Or, "I just need *one good throw* of the cubes to get back in it." But, you know how wild and uncooperative those cubes can be.

Or even maybe secretly she *despises* our neighbors and hopes she can just *cream* them in this so they won't consider coming over again. Not a bad thought actually, but I believe there's other stuff going on here.

Sometimes it's the fault of the *rules* too. If the rules should happen to say that you gotta keep playing until someone squashes the other, then "squash" it shall be! And you can even defend yourself in an innocent, angelic kind of way. "Hey, don't look at me. I *had* to do it you. Those are the *rules*."

That's pretty convenient, don't you think! It gives someone else *all* the summer houses, winter houses, vacation houses, and hotel retreats, but then there's nothing quite like cornering the market! After all, once the prices zoom up to stratospheric levels because of your monopolistic domination, you can then always "sell" a few back to the dejected homeless losers at super-inflated prices in a Good Samaritan type of public relations move. That makes me think that our greedy neighbor will probably be back knocking on the door in about two weeks with a big, cheesy smile on his face. I wonder how he likes sharp, pointy teeth marks in his ankles or red stripes up and down his lower legs?

Look, don't worry about all this. It *has* to be that way. That's just the way you are—born and bred to compete. A tiger in the tank. I think I told you that I've observed the "man owner" watching the sweaty stuff on t.v. and what kind of reactions can be expected if he happened to side with the winners or the losers. But, how do you think he would react if one of his favorite games ended in a "tie"? Thank the heavens that's not possible, huh! That'd probably be like the end of life as we know it!

That's why overtime, extra innings, and extra holes were invented. They bring about a final resolution—appropriately called "sudden death" at times—because without that, it'd be pandemonium! Who would you give the check and trophy to? Remember—there's only *one* big one and *one* super cool one. You just can't hand out the *same thing* to both, can you? It wouldn't *look* right. It wouldn't *feel* right. It wouldn't be right!

The logical and rational thing in this "tieing situation" would be to arrive at the conclusion that *both* teams or individuals played so well that they *both* won. The problem is, neither one feels fully satisfied with this "funny ending," so the theoretically possible win-win situation starts sounding and looking and feeling more and more like a lose-lose finale. And so it is.

You ever seen one of those *soccer* games that, after ninety minutes of running back-n-forth and back-n-forth and back-n-forth and back-n-forth, the final scoreboard reads 0-0 or 1-1? "Now that's a thriller, isn't it! Wow, I could've watched the paint dry instead!" That's what my owner said the one and only time he tuned into one of those events. He now zooms past those things non-stop just like he does with commercials.

Well, I've a got a *true* win-win situation for you—Snowball's coming over again today! I think we'll just hang out around my house this time. I'd rather not risk meeting up with that UFO at the park again, or have to deal with those fat, floating birds down by the pond. Besides, with all that counterfeit dough around here last night, maybe it's best I not show my face out in the open for a few days until things cool down.

I've got it all planned out. We'll have great fun—*cat* fun and entertainment.

First, I'll invite her to partake in a little "cat hockey." No, it's not like the *human* hockey where they skate like flying wizards and beat the living daylights out of each other from time to time. We don't even keep score in our game. (That takes care of the "winner-loser" problem, doesn't it!)

The first objective is to find an object that serves as a puck. We're not too picky as far as that goes, as most anything that will shoot across the floor in an uncontrolled fashion will do. I of course have my personal favorites though.

Like when the "lady owner" leaves her earrings lying on the countertop in the kitchen. Those shiny, slick little devils are just perfect when encouraged to go down onto the smooth floor. Just the slightest sideways paw action will send them skidding unpredictably across the room for some exciting chasing and scampering about!

The usual unequivocal signal that the game's over is when they go hide under the refrigerator and don't come out again. I always wait awhile, patiently, thinking that at any moment the action will resume as they might dare to make another appearance. They never do. I guess that's where they've located the locker rooms, and once they go in, they never come out.

It can be sort of anti-climatic if they get tired early on in the game. Depending on my mood, this sudden turn of events could even bring one of those, deep, slow, elongated meows out of me to clearly express my thorough disgust.

Another great puck for cat hockey can be pens—especially metal ones. They're just so smooth and cylindrical and, unlike the earrings, get some interesting, wild spinning action going if given a good swat on one of their ends.

I have, well "had," this favorite one that the "man owner" used to leave lay out in the kitchen in the evenings when he returned home from work. I heard it referred to as a *Mont Blanc*, but even to this day, I still think it was just a pen.

Anyway, it was a nice, fat one that was great for rocketing back and forth across the floor because with its size and the way it was polished, it was easier to spot, pounce on, and send flying about again.

I remember I was into full-scale competition one evening, looking like a seasoned professional at the peak of his career, and in comes the "man owner." He soon sees what I'm doing and so I'm of course getting ready subconsciously for a heaping of praise and admiration for my active display of talents.

Instead, with a look of horror on his face, he shouts out, "*No*, Fuzzy! Not my *Mont Blanc!*"

I just kept on playing because not knowing what a "Mont Blanc" was, I could at least see that it was just me and this "pen" down here in the kitchen arena. Who knows what he was talking about!

Seeing that, he raced over and right in mid-game during the heat of battle, he snapped up my puck and began to nervously examine every little part of its long body.

"Oh, you've scratched it all up, Fuzzy! Why did you have to do that? Just look at what you've done!"

"Well *of course* there are going to be a few *injuries* from time to time!", I retorted. "That just goes with the game! Haven't you seen all the guys that are missing *teeth* on the *television* version of this sport? What's a few scratches here and there!"

I don't think he understood or made the proper association as he shooed me out of the kitchen with his foot—a most unpleasant and uncultured response—and went on moaning and groaning about the injuries I had inflicted on the puck. I guess he's just a really *sensitive* kind of creature deep down and has some hidden tendencies for non-violent competition.

After cat hockey, I've got some carpet clawing planned out for Snowball and me. That'll be our second form of entertainment for the day as I know that's always a winner at any time.

Personally, I prefer to head up to the long hallway of the second floor of my house. It's sort of like an airplane runway where you can just take off like the dickens and come to a perfect four-point stop at the end and then go into some unbridled fiber yanking.

When Snowball and I do this together, it sometimes leads into what we call the "springy-paw, hunched-back dance"—where we joyously circle around each other all jelly-legged and arched up, clawing with the utmost concentration a small, defined area with our specially developed fluffing skills.

That's really all we're trying to do. You see, sometimes the carpet clawing is directly related to the sharpening of our pointy little weapons, but that's not usually the case since wooden furniture legs and any kind of wooden cabinet really serve that purpose better.

When I need a good, sharp point, I go straight to the dining room chairs and let one of them have a nice, intense scratching. I think they like it and besides, it adds a nice, artistic and personalized decorative touch to my furniture. Consider it as Fuzzy's improvement on an otherwise dull, boring, smoothly finished chair. Abstract art that Picasso would've been proud of!

As I was beginning to explain, "fluffing" is the real intention when it comes to the carpet. As time goes by, the stuff gets all matted down because the "owners" are these big, heavy beings that just walk all over this interior ground cover with their pounding, loping steps and never do anything to do lift it back up again. They run around with that sucking machine I told you about that lives in the closet, but it's more concerned with eating than unmatting. A dusty, ravenous trip around the house, that is, but I still like the fantastic purring sound it makes!

Okay. Having finished our carpet fun, next Snowball and I can entertain ourselves with a little "water bowl adventure game." This can be done alone or with a friend, so it's very versatile and open to one's pleasure at any time. I suppose I'll have to explain this to you humans too because you just aren't brought up learning how to play these rather exciting and exotic games like we cats are.

It's like this. You saunter over to the big water bowl that the "owners" leave out for you. "Sauntering" is okay because I've never seen this object suspiciously move around like the renegade leaves, dust clumps, and other unpredictable household inhabitants. Thus, you can approach it with a certain air of confidence and tranquillity. If it ever should jump up on you—that'd be the day, wouldn't it! Keep precautionary thoughts like that in the back of your mind, just in case, because this is a very big and strange world we're living in. You never know...

All the time you're walking up to it, be looking for something on the path heading towards it that's fairly light, small, and most likely, floatable. For example, a little piece of orphan yarn would do just fine. Grab it up in your mouth and carry it along with you.

Upon arriving at the water bowl, drop in the object and see what happens. If it floats, the fun can begin. If not, repeat the last step and come back with something else in your mouth.

You see, floating objects in water represents a nice, little dexterity game for we cats—as long as they aren't some lunatic, fat birds that are too lazy and stupid to try to fly away like other species of their kind. That's still bothering me a lot, I have to tell ya.

The object of the game is, after releasing the yarn (in this case) into its liquid prison, you try ever-so-gently to lift and rescue the little landlubber out of the water and back to safe, dry ground anywhere around the dish—all the time minimizing the water spilled and keeping your paw as dry as possible. If you're playing this with Snowball, then you take turns at it until the yarn is freed.

It's a lot trickier than you might think because simultaneously grabbing, lifting, and throwing a very volatile and wily object like that—while avoiding the wet stuff—takes years of practice from the time you're a kitty. Bigger objects, like floating leaf boats, are even more difficult to deal with.

This is quite obviously a *skills* game that you play both for fun and to sharpen your reflexes and reactive abilities. All this can come in useful for other required tasks later on in the day, which brings me to our next and last planned amusement of Snowball's visit.

I like this one a lot. There's no real super set of abilities necessary here nor any high level of reasoning or thinking involved to carry it out to satisfaction. Quite simply, this is just pure and natural fun, and for that reason, I've saved it for last. That way, Snowball will leave with a good feeling at the end of the day and my carefully planned efforts will have been a complete and overwhelming success.

I've heard this game referred to by different names by different cats, but I've always called it "window-screen hanging." It's a good, clear designation that gives you an immediate visual image of what we're about to do.

No real tough rules to follow in this case. First, you need to locate a window that's within fairly easy jumping height, unless there's some furniture down around below that will give you a platform to boost yourself up on.

Second, the window has to be *open*, as I've learned through a few failed attempts when this was not the case. You see, if the window is closed, as far as one can tell the screen is still there anyway and it looks like you can begin the game. You make a flying leap and just end up crashing into the glass and sliding uncontrollably down the pane like something I see on the face of that little neighbor boy human next door who's getting headcolds all the time. Disgusting! I meant the window pane. The boy's gotta deal with his own problems.

Third, the open window has to have a *screen* behind it, as I've again learned through a few failed attempts when this was not the case! In this situation, if one gets too excited about playing before checking out all the little details, serious problems can definitely arise. Don't tell anyone this, but I've occasionally run over quickly to an open window assuming there'd be a screen behind it, took a flying leap, and whoaaaaaa! Before I knew it, I was airborne and crashing to the ground below like so much dead weight. Luckily, I always landed on all fours. That's a special cat kind of talent, don't you know?

The four-point, paws down, head up landing is a tremendous genetic engineering feat that I don't believe is fully appreciated among the humans and even the other planetary species. Think about it a little. Get any human to jump head first out of a window like I was just describing and see what happens. I'll bet you that nine times out of ten, he plops down like a pumpkin being heaved off the front porch. Oooh, that's sort of a gruesome image, isn't it. See what I mean though!

Or how about a dog? Try something easy like dropping one of them straight down to the ground from a fairly short height up in the air and the poor mutt's feet just about fold up under him! He'll lie there scrunched up on the floor with a look of surprise and shock on his face, wondering if he's ever going to have the willpower or legs to walk again! No spring action, that's the problem.

This super-amazing, genetically engineered design centers in part around that advanced spring action being built into the legs of us cats. When we land from any position or any height, it's boing, boing, boing, boing. Like highly developed shock-absorbers that'd make a Ferrari squeal for pleasure if it had anything near that level of sophistication strapped on behind its wheels! Yeah, eat your hearts out, you metal boxes you!

The second ingredient in our superior landing abilities results from the incredible balance we have. I'm not bragging here, okay? Just spelling out the facts of the matter for you. "Balance" is a wonderful thing. In our case, we've got little sensors hidden under the skin in the back of our necks that keep us informed at all times as to "which way is up"; in other words, how to maintain an upright position. Should we start to lose equilibrium for any reason, an electronic signal is immediately sent to the brain that puts our whole body on alert status. Eyes are widened, legs pulled back, spring mechanisms tensed, ears flattened—"all systems go" for swiftly correcting the imbalance and creating a soft, stylized landing. (Never leave out "style," when at all possible!) In brief, a fine-tuned piece of systems engineering that NASA couldn't even get on the drawing board, let alone develop and implement!

Finally, the third and perhaps most important factor in our tremendous landing abilities can be summed up in two simple words—No fear! The circumstances be what they may, fall from where we might fall, we simply take it all in stride with the confidence of experience and the innate bravery and valor like that seen in no other living thing in the entire universe. Running through our very veins is the assured thought that *we will prevail*! Now how could any cat land upside down or flat footed with all that going for him! It just couldn't, and doesn't, happen!

I have the feeling I've gotten off the subject here. Well, at least I hope you have a better appreciation for cats now, if you didn't have already before I started. There's a lot more going on than just a super attractive build and a lot of soft fur. You gotta go behind the scenes to get the real scoop at times!

I believe we were talking about "window-screen hanging," weren't we? And we got through the steps of the "approach," "window open," "screen hung" sequence, right?

The last and final step is the game itself. You take a flying leap with all fours with the simple objective of pegging yourself flat against the screen with your claws. And then you just hang there awhile, looking around at the sights inside and outside your house, while enjoying that "suspended animation" kind of feeling.

It's great fun! The view is good, and you get that "I'm in control" kind of sensation that tingles through your whole body.

There's a minor problem in getting loose sometimes if you get your claws dug way into the screen thing and wrapped tight around the wires, but this is nothing a little force and creative redesign of the screen pattern itself won't cure. I've found that the screens are reasonably stretchable and moldable if enough strength is applied.

Hey, I see Snowball coming up the yard in front. Lucky I got the day's entertainment all planned out. Don't tell her about any of my ideas, okay, because I want them to be a surprise. Females like those kinds of things, I've come to learn.

Well, I take that back. I think it depends a little, or maybe a lot, on the *kind* of surprise you've got planned for the female.

You wouldn't believe what happened one time when the "man owner" had planned this big, elaborate surprise for the "lady owner." I'll always remember that day clearly in my mind! I think I've got time to tell ya before Snowball gets up to the porch because she's weaving and circling around, as is appropriate in *my territory.*

I suppose the "man owner" had been planning this whole thing out for a *long time.* This was fairly evident by the huge disappointment etched on his face when it fell through like a bomb at the time of its grand announcement. Body language, you know. I could see the "failure" written all over his face.

It happened after they had gotten home from work one evening, both tired and stressed out from whatever they do all day long. This "work" thing must be a real drag, but that's another story and I'll try to keep focused here since my time is limited.

The "man owner" looked particularly tense that night, like he had something more on his mind than usual. This all goes back to the "thinking too much" problem that I was trying to explain earlier, but I didn't say anything to him since I was being completely ignored in his distracted state.

They sat down in the dining room to eat dinner and I, fulfilling my cat obligation of "floor patrol," was ever vigilant so as to be able to quickly attack, sniff, and if appetizing, *eat* any daring morsel trying to make its escape from the table. It was a dirty job, but someone had to do it!

They went from the salad to the main course, and the main course to the dessert—all with a rather abbreviated and mundane conversation between the two of them. I was getting bored and almost dozing off a little in my upright sitting position because nothing was jumping off the table and heading down my way.

Some nights are like that and you never know when, but you've gotta show up punctually and regularly so as to not miss out on the active ones. It's either "feast or famine," as the saying goes.

Finally, when dessert had been finished, I saw that the "lady owner" was about to get up from her place. They have *places*, you know, and these are sacred sitting locations that no one else even dare think about occupying without causing a psychological trauma that could last days or even weeks.

I saw it happen once. They had "guests" over. The "man owner" invited them to take a seat at the table—I believe with the intention of heading them toward certain chairs because he was starting to do the "traffic directing movements" with his hands. But, before he had the chance, these insensitive creatures just plopped themselves down on the first thing that they came up to!

I knew there was going to be trouble because one of them had occupied what was normally the "lady owner's" chair—her *place*—and when she came out of the kitchen, you shoulda seen the look on her face!

Amazingly, she kept her cool, at least verbally, and didn't scorn the mean, invading "man guest" who was clearly violating her territorial domain. She sat down in another, unmarked, normally unused "place" with this awkward, painful smile pasted on her face that made you think she was about to burst into pieces from the inside out.

All through dinner she could hardly eat, as she kept glancing over nervously at the gloating, insensitive human that was taking full advantage of her usual post. I'd never seen her serve through all the courses of a dinner so fast in my life, but as soon as the desserts had been devoured, she whisked them off to the living room with their coffees, arriving well in front of the "guest invaders" and seating them "appropriately" this time around. The poor "man owner" got a tongue lashing that night when the others went home!

Okay, back to the original story. The "lady owner" was about to get up when the "man owner" caught site of her intended movement and decided to halt her in her tracks.

"Honey, why don't you wait a little before we straighten things up in the kitchen. I've got a special *surprise* for you, and I guess this is as good of a time as any to tell you!"

"Oh, really!" She was obviously delighted and curious at the same time. Okay, I'll hang around a bit for a little human sensitivity session. You don't see much of it nowadays, so better to take advantage whenever you can.

"Well, I know you've been working hard—actually, we've *both* been working hard lately—and I thought it would do us both good just to get away from it all for a little while. I mean, change environments. Change our routine. Do something really different and fun!"

So far, so good, for what I could see. If they both get into a *really good mood* as a result of all this, this could mean "Fuzzy treats" tonight! After all, it had been a dull dinner.

"Hey!", I meowed to the "lady owner." "I *helped* the 'man owner' put this whole surprise together, don't you know! He probably will forget to mention that, but my role was *key* in your upcoming happiness. And I was *pleased* to do it because nothing is too good for the people I share my house with! Don't forget about me down here!"

The "lady owner" was really intrigued now and said, "Okay, go on. Tell me! Don't keep me in suspense!"

Well, that was the beginning of the end, I'm sorry to say—and just after I had implicated myself in this plan! Rotten luck.

The "man owner," with a wide and sincere smile on his face, blurted out, "I got us *Super Bowl* tickets! We're going to the *Super Bowl*!"

This initially perked me up because I knew all about "bowls"—things that *food* come in—and anything called a "*super* bowl" must definitely contain some "*super* food"! That's the logical conclusion, right?

I figured someone had some special event programmed where all the participants would get served these unimaginable delicacies in these huge bowls and all could eat and eat and eat to their heart's content!

"Hey! Did you get *three* tickets by any chance? If not, do you think they're still for sale? I'll go! I might even take a *bath* if you let me in on this one! Come on, you can't leave your beloved Fuzzy out of this event!"

Suddenly, I saw the strangest look come over the "lady owner's" face. Super duper negative body language vibes that'd turn the best party into a funeral atmosphere.

"The *Super Bowl*! How much did you spend on that?"

The "man owner," who had miraculously tuned in to the tremendously scary expression I had seen on her face too, nervously stuttered, "Well, dear, I got the 'deluxe package'."

"That's just great! And what exactly is the '*deluxe* package'?"

"It's, a, well, a, it includes first-class air tickets, an executive suite in a five-star hotel, and a chauffeured limousine to and from the stadium where the event takes place. We've got seats on the 50 yard line."

I was getting the distinct impression that this had nothing to do with a banquet dinner party and there was absolutely no eating involved here. If that's the case, maybe he had really goofed up on this "super bowl" thing after all!

"You did *all* that, without even *asking* me, knowing full and well that I *hate football!*"

Oops! Now I get it. I think this would be the perfect time for me to make my exit. I can see that I'm not really needed around here any more, and best they get this little "mix up" worked out on their own. Besides, I can see that there's no way this is going to lead to any "Fuzzy treats" tonight!

Wow, what a disaster, huh! Just goes to show ya that even "surprises" can be tricky things to formulate and carry out. The best laid plans...

Anyway, Snowball is climbing up the steps now and I'd better get outside. Wow, she's looking as slinky as ever! That's one fine, female feline I'm going out with!

We did the proper greeting, "finger-painted" the front porch again—more out of habit than anything else, and sort of like *our* thing that we do together—and then strolled on into the living room.

After some casual conversation, I suggested we partake in a little "cat hockey" together. The big smile on her face accompanied by the faint purring from deep within let me know that I was right on target for the day. No "false surprises" on my part. We headed off toward the kitchen to locate a suitable puck, soon to *let the good times roll!*

Utopias for utopians

Chapter Seven

"Perfect! Just perfect!" You've heard that a lot, haven't you? Or maybe, you haven't heard it enough, as the case may be. It all depends on your point of view.

If you don't fall for that line every time someone temporarily excited and enthralled blurts it out, then you've probably heard it too much. It's just not believable and as such, loses a little more of its credibility with each mundane repetition.

On the other hand, if you're one of those "eternally cheery optimists" who takes in this kind of stuff as seriously as others may take their cookie-dunking in a glass of milk, then you probably are thinking that this phrase doesn't get expressed with anywhere near the frequency it should.

The real question here centers around how you deal with the concept of "perfect" on both a physical and emotional level. The *basic* understanding around planet earth is that we're dealing with something "without flaws." But "basic" anythings, as we know, never really were of much use to anybody because they just get your feet wet, leaving the rest of the body high and dry.

So what's a "flaw" anyway? That's what I'd *really* like to know. If we understood those things and knew precisely how and when to spot them, then we'd clearly understand the topic at hand. Zero flaws? No flaws at all? Zippo? Nil? Must be perfect!

I've been trying to learn through observation, but quite frankly, haven't had much luck. In fact, the more I observe, it seems the less I understand. A blatantly frustrating kind of investigative endeavor, I'd say!

Like the other day when the "lady owner" had a bunch of other "neighbor lady owners" over to my house. In they came, one by one, and with each new participant that was added, the noise level got louder and louder until I thought I was going to be jabbered right out of my skin.

I had had a nap planned, but with all that high-spirited commotion going on, I had no choice but to tune in and listen up. Complete and total involuntary eavesdropping.

The subjects changed so fast and ruthlessly that I thought I was going to get a real serious cramp in my brain, but I tried to keep up and managed to at least somewhat follow the twisting, turning leaps of that special logic of the communal gossip session. No cat deserves that kind of torture!

"Oh, Betty. Did you hear about what Mabel got herself into? That *poor* woman."

"Well, she would've *never* gotten herself into anything if she hadn't bought that *new car* that she didn't really need. And driving a little *sports* car like that at *her* age!"

So what's the *car* got to do with anything? Is Mabel maybe just an *aspiring* athlete, so she shouldn't be driving that kind of...

"I don't know, but it started *long* before she got the *sports* car. I think she was depressed or upset about something else."

Hey, we don't need the whole history here! I still want to know what she got herself into? Skip the *car* part too, huh.

"You know, Henrietta, that makes me think of that new neighbor Jill down the street. She really thinks she's something, doesn't she!"

Jill? What happened to Mabel? Finish the Mabel story, will ya!

"Oh I've heard about *her*! Maybe we should go down to introduce ourselves some day so we can see what her house looks like inside. I've heard too that she's got *some* air of superiority about her!"

And Mabel? Mabel? What about Mabel?

"So what'd you cook for dinner last night, Betty?"

Now you're blowing off Jill in mid-conversation too! Why can't you...did you say "dinner"? Okay, let's roll with the food topic for a while.

"I cooked the most fantastic pot roast with all the fixings—and you know I don't cook much anymore because of my sensitive back."

Yeah, right!

"But, I decided to do something special, you know. When my Jim got home, what do you think happened?"

"I can just imagine, if a *man* is involved, but go ahead and tell us anyway, Betty!"

"Well, he was *tired* because he supposedly had had a tough day adding up numbers or something, and as if that weren't enough, had eaten a late lunch and just wasn't hungry at all!"

"I can believe it! They don't know what *tired* is. I tell you, I work longer hours than Al most days, and he still expects me to put on a full meal for him!"

"So where are you working nowadays? Didn't you change jobs?"

Jobs? How about a few more details on the *dinner*? Like leftovers for kitties, table scraps, pictures and detailed descriptions of the roast.

"Yes, but this one is just as bad as the other. Lots of work, little pay, and no appreciation for the effort you put into it!"

"Speaking of working, did you see what happened on the soap yesterday? Martha got fired!"

"No! She'd been there for *years*!"

So who in the devil is *Martha* and what does *soap* have to do with anything? Was she too *clean* or something—probably too many *baths*—and made everybody else look bad and that's why they canned her?

"The same thing happened to my uncle Freddie back in the 1970s, believe it or not."

"By the way, that reminds me, the Fosters had their new baby last week and named him 'Freddie.' He's just as cute as can be, though his ears do sort of stand out like satellite dishes! I suppose he'll grow out of that. He's their seventh!"

Is Martha Freddie's mother or what? Maybe she was *soaping* up the baby when...*seventh*! Seven human midgets in *one* "owner's" house all at the same time! Imagine what...

"Yes, some people just get sort of carried away as far as I'm concerned. Like my Aunt Elizabeth and her shoe collection. That woman! I think she's got a pair of shoes for every day of the year!"

Shoes? Okay, now we're on the subject of shoes!

"Well, at least she can't say she doesn't have anything to wear! I'd be happy just to have a pair for every day of the *week*, let alone year. Bob invests all our money in power tools!"

"Yeah, I know what you mean. Like they're some great handy-men or something! We had a plumbing problem the other day, and with a garage full of who knows what, the first thing Frank does is look up a plumber in the Yellow Pages and give him a call!"

I once made some pages *yellow* and got into a whole bunch of trouble! It was late at night, and I...

"And how they charge nowadays!"

"Don't you know it. In fact, speaking of "charging," did you see what they did to the price of melons at the supermarket! Do they think they're selling *gold* or something?"

I'm getting dizzy. If I don't get out of here *now*, I may never be the same again. Okay, I'll try to walk. My head is spinning round and round. I'll just slink in behind the steps and bury my head and body under that blanket. That oughta muffle out the sound enough for me to recover in a couple of years.

I managed to get my senses back about me, but believe it or not, that conversation went on for *three more hours* like that! The most I could get out of it was that there was at least some little thing wrong with every*thing* and every*body*.

How could that be? As far as I could tell by what I'd heard, the whole world was *flawed* in one way or another!

Prices were too high, work was too hard, people had too many shoes and tools, babies were born ready for celestial transmission—there was no end to it! Are things really that messed up?

My personal feeling is that it's all gotta do with "attitude." You see, my great grandmother cat I think was trying to explain it all to me one day in a round-about, backwards kind of way. I was just a kitty so didn't really catch on to what she was saying at the moment, but I've often recalled that story when times like this have come up. That wily, old feline really had a good grip on certain things, I realize now. They say *wisdom* comes with age although I haven't necessarily seen much of that around either as of late—aged or not!

Anyway, it seems that once upon a time there was this cat named Searcher who had always striven for perfection in everything he did. It didn't matter what it was—big or small—he had to be *perfect* at it.

He couldn't just "jump" over a wall, he had to "glide" over it like a floating acrobat. He didn't just walk across his territory, he had to elegantly stroll along, being sure that his musculature was in full and fine form with every step. He didn't just give himself a tongue bath, he methodically and meticulously cleaned his entire body—section by section—in a preordained and strategically planned fashion. He couldn't just run up to his little food bowl and gobble down the contents, he carefully selected and then gently lifted each morsel, one by one, until his dish was left wishing it could offer him more so as to be able to continue on a little longer with such a patient, pleasing experience.

And so on it went. Day after day, activity after activity, Searcher was constantly seeking out new ways and methods to do everything just a little bit better than he had done them before. He was perfecting perfection!

All the other cats around him watched with amazement or envy—or a bit of both—and wished they could be just like him.

"What a cat that Searcher is!", they would say. "What a fine specimen! We should all take note of his unending drive and ambition. We could all learn something from him!"

The years passed by and with each new generation of kitties, the legacy grew and the spectacle went on. Searcher had now reached late mid-age and it was beginning to show—at least physically. Mentally though, he was as tough as ever and continued on his quest to better himself in every way possible and imaginable.

One day, a wild, little, devil-in-his-eyes kitty was scampering light-heartedly down the road when by chance he came upon Searcher's territorial domain. Questioner, as the kitty was called, had never heard of this other great cat's feats nor knew anything about him at all. He really had not been properly trained or cared for by his mother and as a result, without an adequate education early on, was always asking everybody everything so as to try to understand a little more clearly this big, fascinating world he had been born into. "A pest!", they said. "A non-stop, questioning pest!"

As Questioner was bouncing about on the road, pouncing on stray sticks and batting along loose stones, he suddenly caught sight of Searcher strolling across his yard. He stopped dead in his tracks—never having seen another cat walk like that before—and sat down in the middle of the road to watch for a while.

Searcher soon realized that he was being stared at—glared at—and didn't take it too kindly since it had gone well beyond the normal look-and-leave admiration time period.

"Hey, you. Kitty. What are you looking at anyway?"

"At you, Mr. Cat. Why do you walk so *funny* like that?"

"*Funny*! What do you mean, *funny*? There's nothing at all *funny* about the way I walk!"

"But you don't walk like a *normal* cat. You get yourself all tensed up and your muscles sticking out and you look all stiff and uncomfortable and everything and I don't why you just don't relax and walk like the other cats do. Are you sick or something? Don't you feel good?"

"Sick? You said, *sick* or something! Well, I'll have you know that I have spent *years* perfecting this walk and that if you knew anything at all, you would clearly see that this is the most *perfect* walk that a cat could do!"

"I don't know, but it looks really uncomfortable to me! If I tried to walk like that I wouldn't be able to pounce on all these little sticks or bat along all these little stones or have any fun at all! I'd just get all spasm-like and probably just freeze up my whole body right here in the middle of the road! And if I froze up like that, it *really* wouldn't be any fun because then I'd never be able to pounce on all these little..."

"Okay, okay. Don't get started on all that again! And what's all this about 'fun'? Is that all you can think about?"

"Well, sometimes things aren't so fun, like when I fell out of that tree the other day, or when I got one of my paws caught in this mean fence, but most of the time I have lots of fun! What do you do for fun, Mr. Cat?"

"Fun? Well, I, uh, I, well—I don't *worry* about having fun! I am on a quest for *perfection*. I spend my time *improving* myself. Something you might want to think about a little more often, little Kitty!"

"And do you *like* to do that, Mr. Cat? Does that make you *happy*? Are you *happy*, Mr. Cat?"

"Happy? What does *happy* have to do with anything? That's a strange question to be asking me, if I'm *happy* or not!"

"I'm happy when I can go bouncing down a road with all the freedom in the world. I'm happy when my mom licks the back of my head and gets my fur all fluffed up and clean. I'm happy when I get to wrestle with my brothers and sisters and roll around in the grass. What makes you happy, Mr. Cat?"

There was a long, agonizing silence with that last question and after much reflection and consideration on the part of Searcher, he sadly replied, "I don't know, little Kitty. I don't know what makes me happy."

Questioner, figuring that he wasn't going to get anything more out of this conversation, continued his way down the road, leaving Searcher standing motionless and quiet in his front yard. He spent the next three days brooding in his house, hardly eating or getting up to do anything at all. It was like all the wind had been let out of his sails and he could no longer find his desired course, or the energy to get there if he did.

The fourth day, he suddenly lifted himself up and headed out of his territory toward the huge, heavily wooded mountain that lie beyond his town. Rumor had it that a very old and knowledgeable cat inhabited the top of that great earthly monument and that in this feline's mind was stored the wisdom of the ages.

He proceeded valiantly up the rough and difficult trail with a dejected but determined look on his face. Alternating between walking and running so as to maximize his speed without completely dissipating his strength, Searcher finally reached the summit shortly before nightfall. There, sitting peacefully on top of a big, jagged bolder, he saw the old and wise cat that had been said to exist.

"You must be tired, young Cat. You are the first to visit me for many, many years. Come join me on this rock and rest a while. I assume you made this journey looking for me, is that not true?"

"Yes, Mr. Wise Cat.", Searcher humbly replied. "May I ask your name?"

"My name? My name is Utopia. That is who you have been looking for all along, is it not?"

"I don't understand, Mr. Utopia. I don't know what you mean."

"Not *Mr.* Utopia. Just, *Utopia*! Have you not been looking for Utopia inside yourself for all these years? Through your quest for perfection have you not been secretly hoping to really find it someday? To finish your journey? To finally be able to rest, knowing that you had come to the end of the trail?"

"Well, I guess so. Maybe. I suppose *inside* I had thought that, but I just need a little more time. A little more practice. I'm sure that sooner or later I will achieve what you are saying."

"You will achieve *nothing* for there is *nothing to be achieved*! There is no *end* for you because you continue on the road. Only when you stray from the defined path can you realize that you have already arrived. There is no journey to make. You have been *perfect* all along!"

"I, uh, don't know exactly what you're saying."

"Let me ask you this, young Cat. You spent all day toiling up the side of a mountain and at the end of your journey, you found Utopia. Was it everything you were hoping for?"

"Well, actually, no, it wasn't."

"And why not?"

"I guess it wasn't what I was expecting."

"And what were you expecting?"

"I believe I thought that it would make me happy. I came to realize the other day that I really wasn't happy and that I didn't even really know what being happy was like."

When Searcher looked up again, the wise, old cat had disappeared, and in his place, sat the little kitty that he had seen in front of his house a few days ago.

"So, did you find him? Did you find Utopia?"

"Yes, I did."

"No big deal, right! Just an old fuddy-duddy cat with a lot of confusing words, I'd say. You could've spent your time a lot better pouncing on some sticks with me and batting around some stones on the road!"

"You know what—I think you're right."

"Well, it's never too late because there are a lot of sticks and stones all the way down this big ole hill, and if you haven't got anything better to do at the moment, why don't we get after them right now!"

With that, the two cats—old and young—scampered down the mountain instilled with a new, invigorating energy, pouncing on and batting every twig and pebble in sight. All the while, Searcher could be observed with the biggest smile on his face that anyone had ever seen.

So, do you see what I mean about my grandmother cat? She really knew how to tell a story, didn't she! This whole day has sort of worn me out. Too much "mental," if you know what I mean. Gotta keep the "mental" balanced with the "physical" or you just can't maintain the ole motor revving at top speed. That means "tune-up" time and the best way I know of to do that is a nice, long nap. I hope we can talk again on another occasion. It feels good to lie down and rest. I can hardly keep my eyes open. I really need to sleep a while and...

The moment had come. The battle would soon begin as the two forces would clash for what would be a definitive and total victory for one or the other. Fuzzy the Great and his team had completed their preparations of the Chidozer in the wee hours of the morning and moved it into its planned location. All the other cats of the Feline Kingdom had done their utmost to ready themselves for the hideous assault that they would inevitably be forced to face.

There was an air of nervousness and suspense that one could feel dripping off one's very soul, like a thick fog blanketing every nook and cranny of that which it enveloped. The cat citizens had no idea what they should best be doing at this point.

Was it appropriate to go home and rest up their bodies before the onslaught? Should they be eating an extra heavy meal so as to provide them with reinforced energy for what would perhaps be a long and grueling battle? Would it be better to wait in formation and in fighting position so that at the first sign of attack they would be ready to respond?

No one had the answer nor were they expressing their many concerns and doubts verbally to those around them, so most just wandered around the streets in a tense, distracted state of mind.

Fuzzy the Great had long since returned to his castle, alone, and could be found sitting in a meditative posture atop the highest tower that faced toward the direction from which the enemy would come. He remained there, motionless, silent, gazing intermittently out over the catfolk of his Kingdom and then beyond, into the thick, green forest. The blank look on his face gave no clue as to his true emotional state inside. His calm and objective mind would be a key factor in the struggle ahead.

An hour's march away now from the outer limits of the entrance to the Feline Kingdom could be found the thousands of Chihuahua warriors. They had all stopped and stood there in the clearing, tall and proud with the afternoon sun rays glistening off their highly polished body armor and pointy little helmets.

Suddenly, and as if they were all tightly tuned in to exactly the same controlling master mind, every one of the fierce little creatures began to let out the loudest, shrillest, wining noise that you had ever heard in your life. It went on and on as they leaned back and raised their noses to the heavens, announcing the ceremonial speech that their great leader would soon give before their last march to go into battle.

This tremendous howling sound—as if emanating from the

Underworld itself—quickly reached the sensitive ears of all in the Feline Kingdom and sent a shiver of fear through their entire bodies. They did their best to control their emotions, but were quickly overwhelmed by the unconscious images of terror evoked by that invisible, but very audible invader. The attack had begun, and they couldn't even *see* their daring foe. It was a most disconcerting and unnerving tactic.

With a clap of thunder, Chucky the Chihuahua seemed to appear from nowhere and with a vigor fired by a seething and unsatisfied thirst for battle, he rose up high above his followers in grand fashion. He looked so ferocious and domineering that, when lifting his sword triumphantly above his head in a sign of glorious victory, all the other canines raised the pitch and volume of their howling to an even higher level than before. Not so far off in the distance, this left the cats of the Kingdom physically and uncontrollably shaking from nose to tail. It was a sad, dreadful sight for all those who had hoped for the survival of the feline species.

With a wave of his shield, silence reigned once again, and Chucky the Chihuahua began to speak in a snarling, gruesome fashion.

"We have arrived at the doors of our enemy and the threshold of victory, gurrrrrrrrr. Time is short for our *feline fools* for there is no-thing or no-one that can hope to stop us from carrying out our avenging task!"

"You, my Chihuahua soldiers of fortune, will march bravely and relentlessly straight into the heart of the nearby Kingdom, and without hesitation or remorse will let your steely blades find their way to and through their designated targets. And, gurrrrrrrrrrr, you will not stop to rest, eat, drink, or gloat until *each* and *every* *one* of those weak, arrogant, independent-minded cats has met his match, and his fate."

"All but *one*, that is. For *one* is *mine*, and only *mine*, gurrrrrrrrr. This *one* is Fuzzy the Great, for he will fall, and fall quickly, beneath *my* able and avenging sword. And when he falls, this will be the sign, fellow Chihuahuas, gurrrrrrrrrr, of the beginning of the end. The beginning of the reign of a *new master* of these lands, these riches, this domain."

"The *Chihuahua* Kingdom is already etched on the maps and minds of those who know, and who only await the consummation of the inevitable. *We*, gurrrrrrrrr, *will not*, gurrrrrrrrrr, *be denied*, gurrrrrrrrrr, *our destiny!*"

The hideous, ear-piercing howling rose up again with a fervor and energy that shot shock waves through the trees. Chucky the Chihuahua took his position in front of his troops and with high, confident steps, started to lead the ominous procession toward the gates of the Kingdom.

As he did so, he began to sing—at first in a quiet, low voice—and then, with each passing step, a louder, gloating, daring tone that only a fearless warrior assured of victory could possibly think of bellowing out.

One by one, as the howling subsided, the other Chihuahuas followed his lead and soon, their frightful musical announcement of war could be heard throughout the land. Over and over again, they sang,

"The Avenging Chihuahuas are here.
Those warriors whom you most fear.
Heed us, weak felines on the street.
We bring pain, suffering, and defeat!"

At this point, the Feline Kingdom could be found in an emotional state of disarray. As if a horrible, unending, repetitive voice from the Demon himself, the Chihuahua war-march song came emanating from the woods and filled all the town and its inhabitants with an eerie, helpless feeling. They knew the moment had come.

Not one of the cats hid in their houses. Not one of them ran away. This had been *their* Kingdom and *their* land for countless generations past and if it were to be lost this day, then it would be lost by one and all in a valiant struggle of bravery and courage.

Every feline, old and young, male and female, took to the streets in a defensive position. Looking among themselves and seeing that all had come out to offer whatever resistance they could, the cat citizens suddenly began to swell with an energy and self-confidence that fed upon itself and became stronger and stronger with every passing moment.

They were *all* there! One for all and all for one! Strength in unity, victory in mutual support!

Their backs hunched up to the most curved and highest arcs, giving them the powerful appearance of a spring-loaded land warship ready to explode with all its might.

Their tails fluffed out so wide that they appeared to be waving battle axes in fiery defiance behind them.

With muscular legs taut and strong shoulders tense, their pointy-claws were fully extended all round, in anxious anticipation of and preparation for swift, sharp, continuous blows to be delivered to the bodies and faces of their enemies.

And with mouths drawn far back, exposing in all their glory their dangerous, flesh-tearing fangs, they all began to let out the loudest and soul-rattling hissing sounds that had been heard in those parts for many, many years.

At the height of the hissing and with one long, shrieking howl heard from the gates, the Chihuahuas entered the Feline Kingdom. The battle had begun.

It was a terrible sight. The canines came storming through the streets as if there were no end to their lot. The brave felines who encountered the first Avengers fought tooth and nail with the enemy, inflicting great losses on their smaller and weaker opponents in the first hour. They were knocking down their foes and maintaining their defensive positions. In a flying furry of pure and lightening-fast energy, they were standing their ground. For a short time, it appeared the Kingdom may be able to save itself after all.

But, with the passing of time, the cat resistance became weaker and weaker. Wave after wave of the squealing little Chihuahuas continued to flow through every street of the town and as the cats started to tire, the dogs began to find their mark as they lowered their heads and rammed forward with their pointy, little helmets.

Well into the third hour of the battle, the feline resistance force was breaking down. In most of the streets perhaps only half of the original catfolk remained standing and fighting, and in the other passageways, there were few or none left to hold back the unending assault. It appeared that within one or two more hours at most, the bloody and heartless battle would come to a definitive conclusion.

Chucky the Chihuahua had just arrived to the center of the Feline Kingdom and was spinning around in circles in the town square—completely out of control in the extreme level of emotional rage he had worked himself up to. He was a sight to behold—a terrifying, screaming, living incarnation of everything that is dark and evil. He was so caught up in his own internal, angry energy that even his fellow Chihuahuas did not get close to him for fear of their own lives.

Without warning and as if appearing from nowhere, Fuzzy the Great suddenly landed on all fours directly in front of and facing his most savage and bitter opponent. He stood there, tall and calm, his shield gleaming and long sword erect, with an air of confidence and power that could be felt by all those present.

The canine leader stopped his spinning in a flash—having arrived the very moment he had been waiting for—and the two of them, with only a nose's distance separating their warrior bodies, stared deeply into each other's eyes for the longest time. As if pools of illuminating light through long, dark tunnels, the feline could see the burning, avenging hatred deep within Chucky the Chihuahua's soul; and the canine could see the fearless, passionate determination that sprung forth from the inner essence of Fuzzy the Great.

There would be no turning back, and no surrender or recapitulation. Both knew that their destinies were written somehow, in some way, in this soon-to-be historic town square. This would come to be known as the "Battle of the Final Swat."

Word spread like wildfire through the streets that the two leaders had found each other and were about to determine once and for all who would rule from that moment onward. Sporadic fighting continued on in some locations, but the majority of the combatants soon found themselves crowding into the areas around and above the square, waiting with anxious anticipation the dealing of the first blow. An eerie silence had been brought forth among the now bloodied Kingdom, and all knew that this would be the high point of all that had been and all that was to come.

With a quick and powerful movement, Chucky the Chihuahua lunged his shield forward into the shield of his foe, and sent him reeling backwards by the sheer force of the aggression. Seeing Fuzzy the Great off balance and spun around to his side, the fierce canine lowered his head and charged toward his exposed enemy, ramming his pointy helmet through a part of his upper back, just missing the critical spinal bone area.

Taking advantage of the feline's body being temporarily immobilized by the skewering effect, Chucky the Chihuahua spun his great head and body around, hurling the cat across the town square and sending him rolling over the cold, hard stone blocks until he came crashing to a stop against a huge tree at the other end. Fuzzy the Great, seething in pain, had lost his sword in the unexpected airborne flight.

All the other Chihuahuas around the town square lifted their noses to the sky and began to scream and whine with delight. The end would come sooner than they had thought, they could now see. This feline leader truly was a weakling, as they had heard. He was not even worthy to be matched up against his counterpart!

Fuzzy the Great regained his composure and approached his foe with slow, determined paces. All could see that he was in excruciating pain, but he carried himself high and hesitated not.

When the feline got within what was determined to be a swift running distance, the canine lurched out and came charging directly at his weakened foe with his long, deadly sword aimed squarely at his heart. As he was about to strike, the feline suddenly lifted his shield and positioned it at such an angle that the oncoming sword was forced to slide off to the side.

Chucky the Chihuahua, who had been moving at such a speed that gave him no recourse to stop or change directions, found that as the final part of his sword reached the other's shield, it banged his paw with such a blow against the strong, metal, flat surface that he lost his grip—sending the long instrument shooting like an arrow off into the crowd and simultaneously plunging through four of his own dogs.

"Gurrrrrrrrrr! How dare you, cat scum! Look what you have made me do! This is your fault, for your trickery with that shield!"

The canine began to snarl and snap and went into a spinning frenzy once again, losing all control of his emotions. Fuzzy the Great, moving around a bit from side to side, in a deep concentration and as if calculating something with precise detail, suddenly lifted his great shield and wapped the dog upside the head. This broke loose his chin strap and sent his pointy, little helmet flying off and up into the air towards the crowd. It came down like a missile, sharp end first, on the unprotected back of one of the unexpecting Chihuahuas. It was now leader against leader, shield against shield. The odds had been evened.

"Gurrrrrrrrrr! Gurrrrrrrrrr! Gurrrrrrrrrr! What kind of tactic is that, you cowardly, silent cat beast! That is no way to fight, and you have taken another member of my troops with your trickery! You know not the rules of battle nor the ways of proper attack, but I will do you in anyway! You shall pay for you insolence!"

With that, Chucky the Chihuahua threw his shield on the ground to his side, knowing that this armament alone was a rather useless and even silly manner to go about one-to-one mortal combat. Little had he suspected, that was exactly what the feline had been hoping and waiting for.

"Gurrrrrrrrrr! Cat fiend—are you watching and listening? Throw your shield to the ground as I have done, fearing not. Come face me like someone who is at least partially worthy of his species, and we shall determine this match paw-to-paw and fang-to-fang, as it should be! Do you dare to face me as such?"

Fuzzy the Great tossed his shield to his side as his opponent had done, much to the disconcertion of the catfolk gathered round, and with a throbbing, bloody back, formed his body into the best cat attack stance that he could.

The canine leader, limping a bit on one banged-up paw and still feeling a little woozy from the strike of the great shield up against his head, kneeled down in front while loading the powerful spring-action in his huge back legs, snarling and snapping with all his might.

Chucky the Chihuahua attacked a first time, being warded off by a flying front right paw of his opponent. He ran at the feline a second time and managed to grab hold of and rip off a piece of fur on the feline's upper chest, but was sent reeling backwards with a sharp tear in his left ear. A third attempt, using a swift stop-and-start movement, caught the great cat leader off guard for just a moment, allowing the raging Avenger to get a strong grip with his mouth on the other's left front leg.

The canine locked his jaws around the feline's now crumbling leg and shook his head furiously from side to side, sending a shivering through the cats in the crowd as they heard the bones crack and separate.

Fuzzy the Great let out a sorrowful, agonizing howl that could be heard far off into the forest. In a last effort attempt and with all the strength that remained in him, he clamped his fangs as far as he could into the back of the canine's tight, muscular neck. The choking sensation experienced by the dog allowed the feline to break free of the deadly grip. The warrior cat retreated backwards a little as best he was able to on three legs, remaining just out of reach of his furious opponent.

With that encouraging sight, at least from the Chihuahuas' point of view, all the little warrior canines present simultaneously began to sing out in their loudest and most hideous voices,

"The Avenging Chihuahuas are here.
Those warriors whom you most fear.
Heed us, weak felines on the street.
We bring pain, suffering, and defeat!"

The other cats who had gathered around the town square had a look of horror and grief on their faces. If their great leader should soon meet his final blow, this meant that the fighting amongst all who remained would resume. With the dwindled numbers among the feline ranks and the state of exhaustion that they all were experiencing, they knew inside that it would only be a matter of time. Perhaps, a very short time.

Strangely enough, "fear" was not one of the emotions to be found within the catfolk at the moment. More than anything else, they were feeling a deep and profound sense of sorrow.

Sorrow for the apparent soon-to-be defeat of their brave and beloved leader. Sorrow for the loss of their friends and family. Sorrow for the demise of their Kingdom. Sorrow, for sorrow's sake.

Fuzzy the Great was wobbly, and looked down his opponent with clouded yet determined eyes. He was communicating clearly that he was not afraid, and that we was ready for at least one last clash of the titans.

Chucky the Chihuahua, an experienced warrior of many battles, glared at the staggering cat, taking in the details of his much weakened physical and mental state. The blood pumped excitedly through his pounding heart as he prepared himself for what he was sure would be the final assault.

Leaping forward in a snarling fury of sound and motion, he knocked down Fuzzy the Great, sending him rolling over on his back. With everything going exactly as planned—even easier than planned—the canine jumped on top of his motionless opponent, ready to make the last, deadly bite around the other's jugular.

Basking in the glory of his tactics and the howling of the canine crowd around him, he took advantage of the moment to raise his head high and shout out, "Gurrrrrrrrr! As you can see, *we*, the *Chihuahuas*, are the *dominant* species! *We*, the *Chihuahuas*, are the *proper* and *rightful* rulers of this Kingdom! *We*, the *Chihuahuas*, are...*"

Fuzzy the Great, seeing that through the over-confidence and arrogance of the canine leader a small but vital last window of opportunity was being opened up to him, mustered up all the strength that remained in his being and with his good right paw, claws fully extended, landed a tremendous *final swat* across the exposed neck of his foe.

Chucky the Chihuahua, with a shocked and frightful look on his face that sent ripples through every part of his body, stumbled off the feline, moved from side to side for a few seconds, and then fell to the ground.

Fuzzy the Great rolled over and while moaning in pain, got to his feet as fast as he could. He screamed out, "Chidozer!"

That was the signal. All had been carefully trained for this moment, should it come to pass. Every cat remaining ran quickly inside the building to which he had been previously assigned and closed and locked all the doors and windows. This left the Feline Kingdom completely sealed shut, with the exception of the streets.

A huge, ominous-looking mechanical box-like structure—with a big blade in front that had been built to the exact dimensions of the width of the streets—entered into the town square. The expertly trained cats inside the Chidozer were powering its movement and guiding its direction.

All the remaining Chihuahua warriors—who were to be found grouped up in this very location because of their leader's battle—were suddenly being smashed together and bowled over by this "animate, wooden, moving monster" that sent chills of fear through their hearts.

There were sounds of shrieking and screaming in desperation as the scurrying dogs knew neither what was attacking them nor how to defend themselves against such an unknown and unforgiving beast. No songs of glory or victory were to be heard this time around. No defiant expressions of superiority were to be seen. The Avenging Horde of Chihuahuas was on the run!

With a precision and concerted effort that would have made even the most demanding strategist of that time period proud, the Chidozer herded the canines through and out of the gates of the Kingdom. Those few that survived the onslaught went running off whimpering into the woods—never to look back or think of returning to those territories again.

The Chidozer was left outside the entrance gate of the Feline Kingdom, standing as a heartfelt monument to the "Battle of the Final Swat." It would be an important reminder for all generations to come of the bravery and wisdom displayed that day by all who had been present—the survivors, as well as the many who had so selflessly given their lives so that others could carry on.

Fuzzy the Great, in his much deteriorated condition, spent almost six months being nursed back to health by the grateful and caring catfolk of his town.

He slept in specially fluffed up cat beds that contained the finest silk outer cloth and the softest inner stuffing.

He was put through a rehabilitative physical therapy program with specially constructed exotic wooden furniture to be used for intensive scratching exercises.

And, most importantly of all, he was fed specially prepared daily meals of little pieces of cut-up fish that were caught fresh from the mote surrounding his castle.

Yes, life was good, and the Feline Kingdom was safe once again. And they all lived happily ever after.

"Cat Notes"

Happy Memories

"Cat Notes"

"Cat Notes"

"Cat Notes"

"Cat Notes"